BOARDERS AWAY

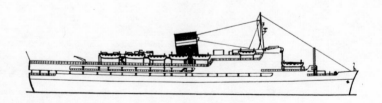

Boarders Away

An account of British India Educational Cruises

with a preface by Sir Ronald Gould
and contributions from Dame Kitty Anderson,
Sir John Wolfenden and
the late Sir John Newsom

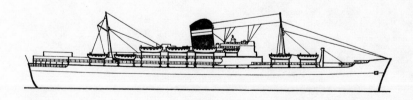

LONGMAN

LONGMAN GROUP LIMITED
London

*Associated companies, branches and
representatives throughout the world*

First published 1973
ISBN 0 582 32471 8

*Printed in Great Britain by
Western Printing Services Ltd, Bristol*

PREFACE

by Sir Ronald Gould
Chairman, since its inception twenty-two years ago, of the Central
Bureau for Educational Visits and Exchanges

For two main reasons I greatly prize the opportunity of writing this
Foreword.

First, it is a privilege to be associated, even if only in a minor way,
with a publication originally the idea of my old friend John Newsom.
Unhappily he did not live to see it completed but this book, now
published, is but one further tribute to a passionately believing friend
of children and teachers.

Secondly, it is a privilege to be associated with this book, because
it is a description and an analysis, appreciative in parts yet critical in
others, of one of the greatest developments in educational travel, a
topic with which I have been associated all my adult life.

In 1923, when I was a student in Westminster Training College,
I was sent for school practice to Ellerslie Road School, Shepherds
Bush, where I was given my first insight into educational travel, and
became an enthusiastic convert. The Headmaster of this school,
Mr G. G. Lewis was one of the pioneers of the school journey movement. He was strongly supported by Mr W. S. Birkett, one of his
assistants, who helped me considerably in my school practice, who
subsequently became H.M.I. in Somerset where I was teaching and
later in Hertfordshire, and who remained a personal friend of mine
until his death. Perhaps, in passing, it might be mentioned that the
pioneers of school journeys were not altogether popular amongst their
colleagues and terms like 'toadies', 'blacklegs' and 'traitors' were
freely used.

However, the Ellerslie Road school disregarded these taunts and
pressed on with their school journeys. What impressed me most was
not the actual visit alone but the careful preparation and follow-up.
For these journeys were not intended to be mere holidays; they were
the means by which reality was brought into the teaching of history,
geography, science, mathematics and literature. So twelve months before a visit, preparations began. Guide books, holiday advertisements,
atlases, books of local history and geography, appropriate music, art,
novels and poetry, biographical dictionaries and much else were all
studied so that as much as possible would be known of the district
chosen. And when they arrived at the centre chosen, every place of

significance was visited and records were made. And when they returned home, to make sure everybody fully comprehended what they had seen and studied, the children prepared a cyclostyled booklet of maps, plans, sketches, records and observations. This record was a permanent reminder of the thrills of new educational experiences, and a reminder to parents that school journeys were primarily educational.

I was deeply impressed by all this, and the more so when I questioned children about their journeys. Life had been given new interests and new dimensions. I was impressed, too, by the soundness of the methods used: careful advance preparation, careful use of time and opportunities at the place chosen, careful recapitulation. This reminded me of the old local preacher's method of delivering a sermon. 'First', said he, 'I tells 'em what I'm going to tell 'em. Then I tells 'em. Then I tells 'em what I've told 'em.' This is sound doctrine for teachers as well as preachers.

Alas, when I began teaching, widespread unemployment and its attendant poverty made school journeys of a fortnight's duration impossible, but I did arrange day and half-day trips. Towards the end of the inter-war years, however, a number of teachers (and I amongst them) realising how school journeys abroad could improve the teaching of languages, history and geography, not only advocated such a development but urged the President of the Board of Education to set up a national committee to advise and aid both groups who wished to study abroad, and groups from abroad who wished to study here. The appeal fell on deaf ears.

After the war, however, when the progressive George Tomlinson was Minister of Education and the equally progressive John Maud was Permanent Secretary, a sub-committee of the National Commission for Unesco under my chairmanship recommended the establishment of a Central Bureau for Educational Visits and Exchanges, to stimulate and service visits of all kinds at home and abroad, and this time the advice was gladly accepted. So the Bureau was established, independent, yet wholly financed from Government funds, and I became its Chairman. Since then, in concert with Local Education Authorities, some of whom were initiating their own schemes for foreign travel, vast developments have taken place. Children, students, young workers and adult groups have been enabled to undertake visits abroad and to widen their knowledge of the drama, music, art, architecture, language and culture of others. No doubt greater affluence has aided these developments. No doubt technological change has helped, too, for the aeroplane has made travel to distant lands a possibility. And perhaps in the future (there are signs already) jumbo jets will cheapen travel still further and enable children to travel even farther afield.

But in recent years, one of the greatest imaginative experiments in educational travel was that initiated by British India – ships expressly designed and equipped as floating boarding schools to be used not merely for enjoyment (though that should not be despised) but for serious education. Of the value of that experiment I have no doubt. Children, whose only previous relationships have been within family, school, church and immediate neighbourhood, have had the opportunity of making new relationships with children and teachers from other areas, with the highly skilled British India teachers, with a Ship's Captain and Officers, with an Asian crew, and even, if only casually, with people in Leningrad, Oslo, Tangier, Jerusalem, Delphi, Naples or Ephesus. This in itself is valuable. The strict order and discipline of a ship, combined with the discipline of a boarding school life is another useful experience, for it becomes obvious to all that order and discipline in such conditions and perhaps in others, are essential for safety and well being. And who could doubt that life is richer after contact with the lives and cultures of others? At any rate, I cherish the happiest memories of a school cruise and life for me is the richer for that experience.

I cannot but note, however, that on the voyage those who gained most had been prepared most carefully, and if I could meet some of the children who were with me on the journey, I have no doubt that those who have gained most of all were those who worked hard before, during and after the voyage. The methods adopted by the pioneers of school journeys are still valid. In fact successful teaching is hard work, and it cannot be dodged by using films, overhead projectors, radio, TV, teaching machines, school journeys or any other new method. I do not decry modern aids or modern techniques, but I know that if they are used, as they should be, to make learning more efficient, they involve teachers in more not less work.

So I warmly commend this book. I hope it will stimulate interest in educational visits in general and school cruises in particular. I hope it will persuade more to take part and when they do, to make the cruises even greater educational experiences.

RONALD GOULD
Chairman, Central Bureau
For Educational Visits and
Exchanges
London

DEDICATION

Boarders Away is dedicated to the memory of John Newsom who was editing the book when he died in May 1971 and, as was his wish, to all Party Leaders and Students who have taken part or hope to take part in the future. Chapter 1 is reprinted from his article 'Returning unscathed from Haifa, Rhodes or Tangier', which appeared in *The Times Educational Supplement* on 12 June 1970. His original introduction, the only part of the book he had completed, is now the second chapter. It describes the benefits of educational cruising and was written with *Half our Future*[1] in mind.

The main chapters are the result of help from John Sharpe, Paul Duncan and the staff of British India Steam Navigation Company Limited, now fully integrated with P. & O.; Chief Education Officers, Advisers, Teachers and Pupils some of whom but alas not all are mentioned in the acknowledgements.

It is impossible to do justice to every aspect of educational cruises within the covers of a book and, likewise, it has not been possible to incorporate all the material offered. I apologise for this and for any omissions in the acknowledgements.

In a literary sense the book may be uneven but no apology is made because the final result is part history, part reminiscence and part guide; this in itself reflects the way in which B.I. Educational Cruises – a unique corporate venture – are identified with the work of the schools.

MARY OLLIS
Hertford

1 *Half our Future* (Newsom Report) Report of the Central Advisory Council for Education (England) under the chairmanship of John Newsom, H.M.S.O. 1963.

ACKNOWLEDGEMENTS

The publishers are indebted to Dame Kitty Anderson, D.B.E., Sir Ronald Gould and Sir John Wolfenden, C.B.E. and all others who have contributed ideas and material on which they have freely drawn in the final compilation of this book and from whom it has not always been possible to obtain formal consent; especially to John Sharpe; Commodore B. A. Rogers, O.B.E., D.S.C.; Paul Duncan; Richard Harris; George Hancock; Ena Smith; Rev. Father W. J. Mills; Rev. Rex Oldham and other members of British India staff and chaplains past and present; to Fielden Hughes but for whose initial enthusiasm this book might not have materialised; to Dr Ronald Hope, O.B.E., Director of the Seafarers Education Service and College of the Sea; to Chief Education Officers, Deputies, Administrative and Advisory Staff from Devon, Kent, Renfrewshire, Leeds, Somerset, Surrey, Southampton, Warwickshire, and Hastings County, Ontario; to Heads, Party Leaders and Students from many schools especially Bideford Boys' Grammar School; Queen Elizabeth Girls' Grammar School, Barnet; Prendergast Grammar School, London; the Lepage Girls' School, Bradford; Sondes Place School, Dorking; Finnart Secondary Girls' School, Greenock; Leamington College for Girls; Maidstone Technical High School for Boys; Milton Abbey School, Dorset; Sir Joseph Williamson's Mathematical School, Rochester; Tanners Brook Middle School, Southampton; Ashmore Park Primary School, Wolverhampton; Uplands Junior School, Wolverhampton; to Lionel Joseph, Jonathan Nevitt, Barbara Newsom, Charlotte Roberts and James Platt, Director of the Central Bureau for Educational Visits and Exchanges; to Joan Butler and Stella Lewins for help with the Bibliography; to Valerie Abbott and Jasmine Grieve for typing the manuscript.

We are grateful to the following for permission to reproduce copyright material:

Education for the article 'Education for International Living' by James Platt from *Education* dated 17 September 1971; *The Times* for 'Education for International Living' (24 November 1971) by James Platt; and 'Returning unscathed from Haifa, Rhodes or Tangier' (12 June 1970) by John Newsom, reproduced from *The Times Educational Supplement* by permission.

CONTENTS

1 INTRODUCTION

by the late Sir John Newsom, C.B.E.

'Returning unscathed from Haifa, Rhodes or Tangier'
(reprinted from *The Times Educational Supplement*, 12 June 1970)

The educational cruises organised by British India Steam Navigation have, in the past decade, carried more than 400,000 pupils and some 35,000 teachers to the Mediterranean, the Baltic, West Africa, the Caribbean and the Atlantic islands. The experience is unique on several grounds and, though accounts of the enterprise have frequently been published, I am still surprised at the ignorance of many involved in the national system of education about the scheme.

This ignorance must be based on the magnetic qualities of the wastepaper basket, for British India's promotion material is widely distributed. So, having experienced two cruises at first hand and studied the increasing volume of reports from schools, individual teachers, L.E.A.s and pupils, I add to the literature of, in my opinion, one of the more significant practical developments of what, for want of a better word, I call educational experience.

First of all the administration: every fortnight, in two liners each accommodating 900 to 1,000 pupils, two new comprehensive schools are created, establish a modest identity and disperse to be re-created within twenty-four hours. In some cases 500 children are assembled at Gatwick and flown to Venice on two successive days and replaced by an equivalent number who have disembarked from the *Uganda* or the *Nevasa*. The pupils know only a dozen or so of their fellows and many of the teachers know a smaller number of their colleagues. To both the 'buildings' are strange and the sea a new experience; many of the pupils have never left their parents before.

Second, the educational value to the children – and, for that matter, their teachers: this will obviously vary according to the preparation put in before the voyage; the qualities of individual pupil and teacher. For a minority I guess it is of small value, but for a large majority an unforgettable experience. This is not only to see and experience, even briefly, places and people hitherto only known at second hand: it also makes history and geography a living reality and not a series of inert ideas. But probably the most valued reward is the corporate life of the ship, the combination of skills which makes the whole extraordinary adventure actually work. And all this at virtually no cost to public funds, for the parents pay the £40 to £70 required, and the young

[1] The fares quoted were current at the time of publication of the article in 1970.

people frequently work part-time to contribute in whole or in part during the twelve months before this voyage begins. British India provide free passages for the teachers.

On my cruise, in fifteen days, the fourteen- to seventeen-year-olds went ashore at Tangier, Malta, Haifa, Rhodes, Corfu and Venice. Brief though the experience was they 'smelled' (in every sense) the Mediterranean lands. They saw Arabs and Berbers, Israelis, Greeks and Italians; they visited the fortifications of the Knights Hospitallers, the area from which Hannibal crossed into Spain; Galilee, Nazareth and Jerusalem; they saw the Dead Sea Scrolls and the relics from Masada, and two of the alleged bays visited by St Paul during his Mediterranean journeys.

They saw orange and lemon trees in fruit, olive trees of incredible antiquity in Gethsemane, Souks and Moorish architecture, and the dramatic modern buildings of Israel. And probably the most moving of all, for several days they could see nothing but the 'unplumbed, salt estranging sea' which, at one stage, reached a wind force 10, with consequential effects on balance and stomach.

They passed off Trafalgar, entered Navarino Bay, watched the famous Israeli gunboats at exercise and returned, on one occasion, to the *Uganda* in the ship's boats in the middle of a thunderstorm. They visited bridge and engine room and learnt the peculiar techniques of deck games on an unstable surface.

In addition to their normal teachers they were exposed to the erudition of the permanent educational staff on the ship; they learnt of the sequence of ethnic invasions from Central Asia to the Mediterranean lands, of the diaspora of the Jews, and the founding and survival of the state of Israel, of Ulysses at Korcyra and Ithaca, of Suliman the Magnificent, of sieges at Malta and Rhodes, of Islam's influence on Africa and Europe, and of the contribution of Venice to commerce and crusade.

But possibly the most important thing of all, they learnt to live together in somewhat cramped surroundings, not to be frightened by strange experience, to know their teachers in a different role, to learn that discipline at sea is right and inevitable, but different. They came from every type of secondary school, grammar, secondary modern, comprehensive and special, and they lived together in reasonable accord. They ate well, even when the waters were troubled.

It would be starry eyed to assert that the profit was equally distributed. Some responded more than others, but I saw no more children obviously bored stiff than I have seen in many schools ashore during the past thirty years. As on shore, the quality and devotion of the individual teachers was probably in direct relation to the success or failure of the experience of the pupils for whom they were responsible. Perhaps the teachers learnt as much as their charges of new patterns of life and relationship. Most of them worked much longer hours and under greater stress than normally but, I would guess, the majority would volunteer again. Who would not endure much to sit on the Acropolis at Lindos in the sun?

2 EDUCATIONAL SIGNIFICANCE OF THE SCHEME[1]

And of course it is true that Education can take us all from darkness into light, that is, so long as we are not thinking of actual schools, colleges, courses, examinations, degrees, but have in mind some rather vague dark-in-to-light process that may be called educational
J. B. PRIESTLEY, *Margin Released*, Heinemann Educational

Some months ago an American tourist stood amid the ruins of ancient Ephesus watching groups of secondary school children walking past. The majority were, in the official language of his country, of 'Caucasian' ethnic origin, but some were black and some were brown and a few were yellow; they talked in English, Urdu, Hindi and Malay, and the French of the West Indies, and were clearly united by some organisation. Turning to an Englishman who seemed to be associated with the procession, the tourist commended the imagination which had apparently brought young people from all over the world for a common educational experience but expressed astonishment that they had so converged, and at the planning involved to achieve it. The Englishman accepted his tribute, but pointed out that the pupils all came from Liverpool and would return there in a week's time. The *Uganda* of the British India Steam Navigation Company, with 900 Merseyside young on board, had arrived at Izmir that morning.

The purpose of this book is to describe how this sort of situation has come about, its growth as a unique educational experiment, something of how it works in practice, of its successes and difficulties and its educational significance. It is written primarily for those who have participated or intend to do so, but it could not have been written by any one individual.

The British India Company, who have given every help in the preparation of this book, are not, of course, responsible for any of the views expressed but they are responsible for the notable experience some 400,000 of us have enjoyed in the past decade. Vulcanicity; kibbutzim; white sunlight in Greece; the continental shelf; communism; flying fish; oracles – a haphazard selection of things we may or may not have read about in our school books. If we have seen Stromboli erupting or caught the zeal of young people working in

1 *Editor's Note*: This chapter was written by the late Sir John Newsom in November 1970, in the light of his personal experience and with *Half Our Future* in mind. Much interest is now expressed in cruises for younger children which may be a growth point in the future. References to a middle school programme and to advanced work with more able students are included elsewhere.

Israel; if we have blinked at the glaring light on the Parthenon, felt a great ship surge and fall in the Bay of Biscay or queued in Red Square to see the Lenin Mausoleum; if we have watched the delicate skimming of winged fish over the water or been drowned in the dramatic atmosphere of Delphi – if we have experienced only one of these things we have enriched our lives incalculably. Bringing such experiences into the lives of young people is one way B.I. have changed the face of education. On the other side, the disciplined community life of 'the school at sea' enables young people to learn that living together means consideration for others, putting in rather than taking out, the dignity of comradeship: that 'no man is an island, entire of itself'.

Almost inevitably the concept of a seagoing school is difficult to comprehend. This is especially so if 'education' is defined in the narrow terms of class-room experience geared to a particular syllabus designed to satisfy external examiners. This is a pompous way of describing 'school' solely or mainly concerned with the acquisition of factual knowledge and particular mental and physical skills. Of course this is an important part of the operation but the adequate development of the adolescent young involves a good deal more. A further difficulty is the average emotional response to the word 'cruise'. To most people this implies a 'holiday', the antithesis of 'work', a view supported by much of the glossy promotion material put out by shipping companies to attract custom for this, to be fair, most usual interpretation of the word. Is it possible to 'cruise' and 'work' simultaneously? I believe it is and that the British India Company have demonstrated it beyond doubt.

But this means describing, superficially and briefly, what I believe to be some of the important educational influences that are not necessarily classroom based. It would be superfluous to mention these to teachers with boarding school experience, and for very many whose teaching has been wholly in day schools the school day involves a great deal more than the formal, or informal, work which takes place in laboratory, workshop, gymnasium or playing field. Nevertheless, from observation, this total involvement with the pupil is not universally recognised and, admittedly, some teachers would deny its necessity. During the period thirteen to eighteen the growing-up process which began in early infancy continues even if in altered form and with infinite variety according to physical, and mental attributes, parental and social influence, and the ethos of an individual school. During this period the young should at least be exposed to situations in which personal and group relationships can develop; this means learning how to accept a majority view if one is in a minority and vice versa; it means learning how to live with and exercise authority; it means adjusting oneself to a changing relationship with one's parents, teachers or contemporaries; it means learning values both aesthetic, moral and rational; in short, the mastery of skill as an adult in an adult world, which is different from being a child in a world of childhood.

A few educational cruises are designed for children of primary school age, but the majority are for young people between thirteen and eighteen. In a 'secondary' connotation it is worth quoting one paragraph from *Half our Future*:

The work in a secondary school becomes secondary in character whenever it is concerned, first, with self-conscious thought and judgement; secondly, with the relation of school and the work done there to the world outside of which the pupils form part and of which they are increasingly aware; and, thirdly, with the relation of what is done in school to the future of the pupils, that is to the part they see themselves playing, or can be brought to see themselves as playing in adult life. The first of these characteristics, the quality of self-conscious judgement, differs in kind from the other two. It describes a mental process that involves the use of reason and imagination to bring order into the world of things perceived.

Most teachers would accept this as the assumption on which the value of educational cruises is based. Yet because of the 'hardness of our hearts' British India's promotion activities had originally to be based on a more restricted educational concept; the emphasis was as much on the number and style of class-rooms available and the benefits accruing to particular 'subjects' as on the less easily defined, and admittedly amorphous, concept of a personal experience for an individual pupil. The relatively few teachers who anticipated transferring their land-based four-form entry grammar school to a ship en route from Gibraltar to Malta with no more than a change in its foundations from cement to water, are those who have probably been disappointed by the experience. Those who understood that a fortnight is a desperately short period to make significant a new experience, prepared for it and adapted their plans as occasion necessitated, were probably a trifle exhausted at the end but knew that what had happened to them and their students was, in total, to enrich the lives of both.

Translating these generalities into examples is, over all, a question of transferring indirect to direct experience. It is not the same to be told that Hannibal crossed to Europe by the narrow sea passage between Morocco and Spain as to see with your own eyes how near they are. It is not the same to be told that there is a Mediterranean climate as to experience it in its many vicissitudes, that Malta can be uncomfortably cold, that it can rain heavily in Galilee, that it can be hot in Tetuan in February and the Baltic in August. Even elementary truths become more significant: whole cities are inhabited by people to whom the English language is largely unknown and who yet possess cars and radio; architecture is sensibly adapted to climate; everyone does not wear trousers or, even in 1970, the mini-skirt; the sea can be rough and there is, above all, a lot of it. History books inform that the Moors inhabited Spain for centuries, a variety of Europeans the islands of Rhodes and Malta, that there was 'trouble' in Navarino Bay in 1827, an ancient civilisation in Egypt when our ancestors led a pretty primitive existence, Columbus spent his last days in the 'old' world on several different islands, and that Venice as Wordsworth put it, held 'the gorgeous east in fee', but to see with your own eyes what was previously accepted from book or blackboard or atlas or from the mouths of devoted mentors, this *is* different.

Other things can be learned. Education in Great Britain is still, and will be for a long time to come, experienced by many young people in schools termed 'selective' or 'unselective' with all the social and intellectual divisions involved. Even if this were not the case we differ in many ways and attitudes if we come from north or south, east or west, urban or rural. These cruises, even when all schools come from one Education Authority, mix us up and expose us to a sense of the diversity which exists even in a small group of islands. Sunderland is not the same as Watford, and oddly enough to the English, Glasgow is not the same as Inverness! Even the counties and cities of Wales have marked differences of attitude, let alone language. On one cruise, I discovered girls from a grammar school who shared dormitory accommodation with their contemporaries from a school for the educationally retarded and who did not appreciate the difference until they were told. There is a moral in this story somewhere to be discovered by those wiser than I.

Sadly, there is a division so far unsurmounted but which, one day, might add to the social value of the cruises. For the most part the young people attending schools in the national system of education are separated from the 5 per cent or so in private schools. True, in certain sixth-form cruises there is contact, but otherwise there is separatism in the sense that the private preparatory schools have their own expedition and that the independent secondary schools are only rarely involved. This is not necessarily due to any ill-will. But it would be an advantage if boys and girls from private schools could combine with those from the majority; both would learn from each other and, not least, their teachers.

Schools tend to be communities of teachers and taught; cruise ships have a wider spread. Numerically the young have it but there is the ship's company, officers and ratings, European and Asiatic; there are cabin passengers of all ages and every part of the United Kingdom, and all have a common base, a common interest – the ship. It is facile to be romantic about this, but a ship differs fundamentally, literally, from a hotel, a school, a camp, or a domestic dwelling. It is all these but more, it moves and it is isolated, it is surrounded by a potentially hostile natural force that is uncontrollable by man. Our unity as human beings is, implicitly and explicitly, more manifest. It is interesting and moving to see how quickly the students identify themselves with *Uganda* and *Nevasa* – at the first port of call the ship becomes an element of security, we 'go back home' at the end of the day. Coming 'home' may involve a short passage in the ship's boats for at some ports *Uganda* and *Nevasa* cannot moor alongside. This in itself is an experience, especially in a moderate swell, but I have observed how the fifteen- to seventeen-year-olds are impressed by the manner in which the ship's boats are commanded by young men little older than themselves who, with one member of the Asiatic crew, handle a £5,000 lifeboat with sixty passengers. Qualities are quietly shown which are different from those demonstrated ashore and can be mildly chastening to those to whom leadership has become emotionally a 'dirty word'.

For the tiny minority of young people who are at boarding-school the recurrent departure from home to school environment becomes an accepted rhythm; for the majority at day school this experience is, until late adolescence, unusual or never experienced. Indeed, for a large number of cruise students it represents their first absence from home or, at least, from their parents. Despite the immense growth of school journeys, camps, au pair visits, and so on, during the past twenty years, it is often forgotten how many young people do *not* have this experience, or for how many 'leaving home', even temporarily, is unusual. An educational cruise is a more dramatic departure than most and a total change of environment, but the company of friends eases the transition. None the less, it is an important part of the growing-up process and, even if the more extreme claims of boarding school protagonists are exaggerated, there is no doubt that a short experience away from home is invaluable.

It is sometimes forgotten that the majority of British people never experience 'foreign parts' even though there has been a great change in the past twenty years. Until recently unless in khaki, the average Englishman never left the United Kingdom. Despite package tours to Spain, which are sometimes not much more than carrying his home environment to the sun, there are still hundreds of thousands of our compatriots who have never met an Italian or Scandinavian or a Greek in *his* home environment. Thiry-five years ago when I lived in County Durham there were families in that county who had never seen the sea – so perceptibly we progress.

On several occasions the report *Half our Future* stressed the value of school journeys and residential experience for young people between thirteen and sixteen. It did so because the evidence from the teaching profession overwhelmingly recommended it.

There are, moreover, lessons of wider significance to be learned from the cruises. Although the analogy is not precise it could be said that, every fortnight, *Nevasa* and *Uganda* create a new educational entity of pupils and teachers drawn from every type of school. Some teachers and some pupils have met before, but for many a totally new community comes to life and within forty-eight hours has achieved an identity and achieved it under circumstances novel to all the participants. This is remarkable, but it is due in part to the very fact that to all, of every age and capacity, the experience is unique; everyone starts equal in their inexperience of life at sea and for the majority of the young people it is their first experience of foreign travel.

The speed with which this feeling of belonging becomes apparent is due largely to the expertise of the ship's company, both 'mariner' and 'educational'. They have learned how to create the atmosphere whether it is by the immediate demonstration that life afloat is different from life ashore – Emergency Life-Boat Stations occurs within a couple of hours – by the first conference of party leaders, by the disciplined arrangements necessary to obtain the first meal, or by that indefinable feeling of purposeful activity and efficiency involved in getting a large ship cast off and under way. At any rate, when the first port of call has been made the ship is accepted as 'home' or 'base', the secure focal point in an alien world whether of sea or land. By the end of the cruise it is difficult to believe that students and staff have only been together for a fortnight and that, however evanescent, an identity has been established. The final evening when 900 to 1000 young people gather for a farewell celebration can be deeply moving and not only to the middle-aged spectator – it is evident in the eyes and actions of the young.

In discussing the social and educational significance of educational cruises, it is fitting to show this is sometimes 'got across' to the students in direct and simple terms.

When conditions make it practicable, a united morning service is held for both students and cabin passengers in addition to the more specific denominational services. On a recent cruise the Roman Catholic chaplain delivered a homily based on a quotation from St Paul's Epistle to the Philippians while *Nevasa* was within measurable distance of Philippi.

Let me remind you again of the words of St Paul's letter, which the Captain read a few moments ago. . . . 'If our life in Christ means anything to you, if love can persuade us all, or the Spirit that we have in common, or any tenderness and sympathy, then be united in your convictions and united in your love, with a common purpose and a common mind. Always consider the other person to be better than yourself, so that nobody thinks of his own interests first, but everybody thinks of other people's interests instead.'

These words are a strong appeal for unity by St Paul to the Christians living at Philippi. Even in those early days (the Epistle was written about A.D. 60) divisions threatened the peace of the Church at Philippi, one of the principal cities in Macedonia, today Northern Greece.

These words of St Paul, and this cruise in *Nevasa*, have given me three ideas: first the idea of *Community Living* which makes us aware of our *Social Responsibility* and, in turn, leads to a desire for *Christian Unity*. This may sound a little complicated. In simple language we are going to live together for two weeks as one family on board this ship. Most of the students with whom we are sailing are much like ourselves but there are those who do not always think or act in the same way as ourselves. Whatever we do as individuals there are times when we all have to think and act together for the good of everybody on board. For example, lifeboat drill, ship's rules and safety regulations, not smoking in certain areas of the ship, keeping quiet in the dormitory so that others can sleep, not using transistor radios, going ashore together as a group and not wandering off on our own. Imagine the chaos that would result if an announcement came over the 'Tannoy': 'The first 400 to disembark will go on the morning tour to Athens' – the scramble for the gangway; Party Leaders looking for students, and students looking for party leaders.

Living together has made us think of other people, and what we can do for them; and this is what we call social responsibility.

For many of you, this cruise is the first time that you have attended a service and prayed together with people of other denominations, and some of you may say 'why don't we do more of it at home? Why are there so many different religions? Will the day ever come when we will all be united?' This we call a longing for Christian unity.

I have been coming to sea for six years, and the more I come away, the more I appreciate the tolerance and understanding which seafarers and people who work at sea have for one another and for people in general – and in particular for the passengers for whom they are working.

You have come for a fortnight's Educational Cruise and then you will go back home. But for those who work on board, this ship is their home for most of the year. In another two weeks they will see a new set of faces, students, Party Leaders and cabin passengers, and they will set sail again. By that time, you will have realised to live together peacefully there has got to be 'give and take'. When we live together what we say and what we do has an effect on other people; what they say and do concerns us.

Bearing this in mind, we realise that we have to think about other people as well as thinking of ourselves; and we call this our social responsibility. As St Paul says, we should aim to 'be united in our convictions and in our love, with a common purpose and a common mind'. True love makes us forget about ourselves and think of the good of the people we love. Our Lord has told us 'We must love one another as He has loved us', even those with whom we find it difficult to get on. We can do so much by being kind, by being friendly. If we keep St Paul's words in mind, we will have an ideal to guide us.

Since we are united in our prayer to God here on deck this morning – we think of Christian Unity.

The late Pope John said – 'let us concentrate on what *unites* us, and not on what divides.' What do we have in common; what we *all* believe? If we want to do something positive for Christian Unity, we must pray for it and pray that God will guide us. From prayer will spring the desire to know more about one another's teaching and worship and traditions, a 'dialogue' or discussion between members of different denominations.

Praying and teaching together can lead us to act together, and we find that this is already the case especially in times of trouble and national disaster.

I hope and pray that having lived together as a community afloat, you will leave the ship with the intention of thinking of others before thinking of yourself, of helping others and of praying for Christian Unity.

3 HISTORY OF THE SCHEME

Beating swords into ploughshares

THE ORIGINS

Why an old-established British shipping company, with its roots deep in the Empire of past generations, should have become responsible for an important educational medium attuned to present-day needs and attitudes requires some explanation. The origins of British India Steam Navigation Company Limited, known generally as 'B.I.', go back to 1856 and two Scottish merchants trading in Calcutta, William Mackinnon (subsequently made a baronet) and Robert Mackenzie. These gentlemen secured a Government contract to carry mail from Calcutta to Burma and came back to Scotland to raise the capital and acquire appropriate ships. In doing so they created a liner company which was to become one of the largest in the world.

This new company's first ship *Cape of Good Hope*, on her way to India in 1857, embarked a regiment of British troops at Colombo for passage to Calcutta to assist in the suppression of the Indian mutiny and almost from its birth trooping became a feature of B.I.'s activities – one which was to continue almost without a break for more than a century.

Over seventy years later, following the First World War, the B.I. passenger ships *Neuralia* and *Nevasa* were chartered by the British Government for eight or nine months each year for trooping and, by the custom of that time, were laid up in Southampton Water from May to August preparing for the next trooping season. The majority of these trooping voyages were to India, these were the monsoon months in any case, and it was not considered desirable for soldiers to face the rigours of the Red Sea during the hottest months of the year. Those who recall the mess decks fitted with hammocks in which soldiers then lived and slept will not be altogether surprised at this humane decision.

Mr George White first thought of the idea of using any suitable passenger ship to become available for schoolboy cruises. Mr White, a retired Post Office official living in Edinburgh, secured the interest of the Scottish Secondary Schools Travel Trust which, for some years previously, had arranged overseas visits for schoolboys of member schools. The outcome was the charter of *Neuralia* (9,200 tons) for a voyage to Baltic and Norwegian ports. She sailed from Leith on the 25 July 1932. No conversion of any sort was undertaken. The 1000 or so schoolboys occupied the troop decks used by soldiers and the schoolmasters the cabins used by officers. This fourteen-day cruise to Baltic ports was followed in the same year by the English Secondary Schools Travel Trust, sailing from Hull. Thus was established a practice whereby two schoolboy cruises for these charters took place each year up to and including 1938. The Company's newly built troopship *Dilwara* (12,600 tons) replaced *Neuralia* in 1936. Meanwhile, in 1935 the School Journey Association of London chartered *Nevasa* (9,200 tons) for two similar cruises, transferring in 1938 to *Dunera* (12,700 tons), the latest B.I. troopship. The imminence of war discontinued these cruises, which did not take place in 1939. There was no doubt that they met a need of their time and there was no shortage of schoolboy applicants for accommodation at £5 for fourteen days, even though they occupied cramped quarters and were required to assist in the preparation and service of their own food. These were recreational voyages and no direct attempt was made to use them for educational purposes.

POSTWAR DEVELOPMENTS

Neuralia was sunk off the coast of Italy shortly before the end of World War II and her sister ship *Nevasa*, one of the few British passenger ships to survive both world wars, was withdrawn from service early in 1948 and broken up. In the postwar era, sea trooping was carried on throughout the year and existing troopships were converted to more elaborate and comfortable standards. In 1956 a new *Nevasa* (20,160 tons) was built by B.I. to the Government's latest specification for trooping and was given a charter for fifteen years' continuous operation. There then seemed to be no prospect of reviving the schoolboy cruises of earlier years.

Nearly twenty-three years after the last schoolboy cruise, at 1600 hours on the 12 April 1961, the school ship *Dunera* was piped away from Princes Pier, Greenock with a total of 732 Scottish schoolboys and girls and their sixty teachers, bound for Corunna, Gibraltar and Lisbon on the first British India Educational Cruise.

The preceding six months had been a hectic time for the small B.I. shore staff concerned with the operation of troopships. When in October 1960 the Ministry of Transport indicated that *Dunera's* trooping charter would be terminated in Februrary 1961, B.I. recalled the earlier schoolboy cruises and the few contacts which had remained with the Associations responsible for them. There was no question of retaining a highly specialised and costly passenger ship in service for two or three cruises each year, as no alternative employment for the rest of the year now existed. It was, however, decided to consult these contacts, and Chief Education Officers who might be interested, about the possibility of converting *Dunera* as a school ship for boys and girls for operation throughout the year in holidays and termtime alike. The Ministry of Education had made it clear that the adoption of such a scheme would be entirely a matter for each Local Education Authority and that it was not in any position, under the Education Acts, to make recommendations on a subject of this sort. A meeting was arranged on board *Dunera* at Southampton on 5 November 1960, to which all Chief Education Officers were invited, and also representatives of school travel associations. Of the forty or so people attending this meeting, almost all remembered the schoolboy cruises of prewar days. A number were cautiously enthusiastic about this revolutionary suggestion but obviously they could not commit themselves as to whether there was any real prospect of recruiting up to 16,000 school children, spread over the year, to ensure the economic viability of a project of this nature.

B.I. decided to go ahead – a courageous decision in the light of all the circumstances. Whilst *Dunera* completed her last trooping voyages plans were drawn up for her conversion and tenders for the work were obtained from the shipyards. A programme of cruises running throughout 1961 was worked out and sent to all secondary schools in the country and the reconnaissance of suitable ports of call, including the arrangements for shore excursions, carried out. The programme envisaged a series of ten-day and fourteen-day cruises from major U.K. ports to the Iberian Peninsula, North Africa, the Atlantic Islands and to Norway and the Baltic during the summer months, and fourteen cruises in the Mediterranean, in conjunction with rail transfer to and from Venice, Marseilles and Genoa during the winter. The standard dormitory fares for students were £28 for ten days and £34 for fourteen days. This included free shore excursions at each port.

After disembarking her last soldiers on 8 February 1961, *Dunera* proceeded to Vickers Yard at Hebburn-upon-Tyne and the work of conversion, costing over £100,000, proceeded at once.

A permanent headmaster designated Director of Studies[1] and his deputy were engaged, together with a matron, five assistant matrons, six masters-at-arms, two surgeons and two nursing sisters to assist in welfare and supervision. Cabin accommodation was retained for teaching staff accompanying students and it was considered essential to maintain on board the teacher/student relationship existing in school. Initially teachers were offered places free in the ratio of one to twenty students but this was shortly increased to one to fifteen. A balance of about 100 berths in cabin accommodation, beyond teachers' requirements, was retained, partly to avoid further conversion costs and partly to encourage members of the teaching profession and others concerned with education to travel privately, as fare-paying passengers, thereby spreading interest in the new venture more widely. The retention of this cabin accommodation was to prove of great value and significance in the development of the scheme.

1 In 1962 this title was changed to Director of Education but since 1 October 1971 it has been Headmaster.

By the middle of March it was clear that B.I. would shortly be the owners of a fully equipped school ship manned by an experienced Ship's Company under Captain (later Commodore) B. A. Rogers, O.B.E., D.S.C., totalling 297 officers and ratings. Equally it was evident that only a handful of passengers had been booked for the sixteen cruises planned for the remainder of the year.

Scottish representatives attending the earlier meeting had shown particular enthusiasm and the first two cruises were, therefore, due to sail from Scottish ports. Urgent methods were now necessary to recruit sufficient students to assist in demonstrating an educational concept which the Company was still confident was worth while. All available members of staff went to Scotland. Assisted by the Company's Glasgow and Edinburgh Agents and with the encouragement of a number of Directors of Education for Scottish Counties they made visits to many schools. A 50 per cent rebate in passage money was offered to students taking part in the first five cruises. This enabled *Dunera*'s first cruise to sail from Greenock with 732 students, her second with 768 and her third with 788 (mainly from Northumberland and Newcastle). By the end of 1961 fifteen cruises had been operated; 1,436 cabin passengers and 8,268 dormitory passengers had been carried. One cruise was cancelled through lack of support.

THE 'DUNERA' – MAIDEN VOYAGE

Commodore Rogers has recalled the *Dunera*'s maiden cruise from Greenock:

The ship's sailing and the school ship project generally were given good publicity by press and television. It would have been much greater but for the epic first space voyage of Yuri Gagarin which took place on sailing day. On a later cruise in Athens at the Acropolis a number of students were lucky enough to meet him.

The first morning at sea disclosed a pleasant surprise in the complete absence of the heavy atmosphere below decks so apparent when carrying troops. The rapidity with which students settled down to the shipboard routine after their first night at sea was also most encouraging. Soon the whole set-up was moving forward with an assurance which was revealing itself by the time we reached Corunna, our first port of call. This coincided with a holiday for the local schools and university. As the students disembarked they were met on the quayside by a large crowd of Spanish students. As I watched the mixing of these Spanish and Scottish students within a short distance of the tomb of Sir John Moore I remembered that he was a Glasgow born man whose epic retreat to Corunna had been greatly assisted by the local Spanish people who had fought rearguard actions shoulder to shoulder with Sir John's troops. Was it not probable that research would reveal that the forefathers of some of these young students had fought side by side in 1809? Imagine what a Philip Guedalla or Arthur Bryant would have made of this!

It was a great curtain raiser and revealed what scope for goodwill these cruises would offer and what splendid opportunities our young ambassadors would have of spreading it.

Later, as the school cruises settled down, there were many opportunities for intermixing and as the years passed our ships became very well known and popular at the ports of call.

At each port the student body was divided into two. One division was sent off on an organised coach tour to places of interest while the other went sightseeing and shopping independently. All day coach tours with packed lunches provided were tried in the early stages, but it was found that students much preferred to return on board for the mid-day meal and a wash and brush up before going off again for the afternoon. Thus this general pattern evolved and only exceptionally, when places of interest were far distant, was an all day trip arranged.

It should not be imagined that these coach tours started off perfectly organised, with parties homogeneously seated in the same coach. In fact at the end of the first visit to Corunna the Director of Education told me it was 'an Imperial muck-up'. But he struggled on through endless discussions at party leaders conferences until in all ports of call the coaches were lettered and numbered and parties kept together with their proper leaders. This took months of pleading with coach operators in foreign ports but in the end they got the message that these were not ordinary tourist cruise passengers but students in a schoolship, and the Director finally got his way.

Farther southward at the next port of call, Gibraltar, the excursions had to be arranged in a multitude of taxis as coaches cannot use the narrow roads of the Rock. Later on these excursions were done on foot.

The maiden cruise turned round at Gibraltar and on the run home a call was made at Lisbon. This historically interesting and most beautiful capital city has retained its appeal to the present day and it is very few cruises indeed on the North Atlantic run that do not include Lisbon in the programme. Symbolic to the thoughtful is the large statue of Christ on the south bank of the Tagus opposite Lisbon which, floodlit at night, looks down with arms outstretched towards the ship and the city behind her.

During the run home from Lisbon to Greenock it would have been ordinary practice to shape a direct course from a position west of Cape Finisterre to pass west of the Isles of Scilly and so on northwards to the Irish Sea. Economically sound but lacking in interest this route would not do. A slight deviation to the eastward would enable us to see Ushant, the Wolf Rock and Land's End. It could happen that hazy weather would make this a waste of time but this had to be accepted.

On 25 April 1961 the ship berthed at Greenock. The first cruise was over and, as passengers and students streamed down the disembarkation gangways, one could sense that it had been a success. It was not necessary to ask them, any more than it is necessary to ask a happy family if they are happy.

As cruise followed cruise a fund of experience was slowly built up and improvements in the organisation were introduced. In all this the ship had great support from the Cruising department at Head Office whose work in keeping the ships supplied with students and keeping in touch with the educational world is a success story in itself.

This trial period had proved beyond all question that it was feasible to operate a suitable ship as an educational establishment afloat and that, with first-class administration on board and at ports of call, it offered a worthwhile social and educational experience.

The financial outcome of these early operations was far from encouraging. No subsidies were available and very few Local Education Authorities were prepared to contribute anything towards the children's fares. To operate the *Dunera* economically and retain fares at levels within the means of the majority of parents it was essential to have a high level of bookings for every cruise throughout the year. Although many Local Education Authorities in Scotland were prepared for school groups to travel in termtime this was not then the case in England.

On the other side of the ledger was the tremendous enthusiasm of passengers who had travelled and these included Chairmen of Education Committees, Chief Education Officers and other educationalists who had occupied the 'spare' cabin accommodation and who had declared their future support. Many others were visited by B.I. staff and a number were prepared to accept the evidence of these early *Dunera* cruises.

It is encouraging to read one account by a man who had sailed in the *Dunera* as a member of the armed forces based on the changes of function he noticed in different parts of the ship; where he once slung his hammock in a troopdeck, the children now slept in brightly coloured dormitories; where his platoon had drilled, two teams now engaged in a vigorous game of deck hockey; where defaulters had previously languished in the cells, eager youngsters developed their films in the photographic dark room.

THE 'DEVONIA'

An optimistic feeling prevailed about the future. In February 1962 the Bibby Line troopship, *Devonshire*, became redundant. The only other comparable ship then available was purchased by the Company and converted as a school ship at Barclay Curle's yard on the Clyde. Her capacity and characteristics were identical to those of the *Dunera*. This ship was renamed *Devonia*. She joined the service in April 1962 and undertook twelve cruises during the year. She also made a voyage to Bombay and back, principally to change the Asian crews who manned *Dunera* and *Devonia*. At that time the capacity of the two ships exceeded the demand which had been created up to date but there was a steadily growing interest in future operations. The immediate financial outlook, however, continued to be gloomy. By the end of the year the Company had experienced no return on the substantial capital invested and had also suffered cumulative operating losses.

Table 1 shows that the tide turned in 1963 when *Dunera* and *Devonia* undertook forty-one cruises carrying nearly 31,500 passengers. In

1964 the same number of cruises carried 34,200 passengers and in 1965 the number of passengers increased to over 37,000.

Table 1

calendar year	ships employed	number of cruises	number of cabin passengers			number of dormitory passengers	total
			party leaders	fare paying	total		
1961	Dunera	16	551	885	1436	8268	9704
1962	Dunera/ Devonia	32	982	3142	4124	14731	18855
1963	Dunera/ Devonia	41	1716	4038	5754	25743	31497
1964	Dunera/ Devonia	41	2188	4467	6655	27535	34190
1965	Dunera/ Devonia/ Nevasa (Nov/Dec)	41	2260	4388	6648	30356	37004
1966	Dunera/ Devonia/ Nevasa	53	3430	7696	11126	42824	53950
1967	Dunera/ Devonia/ Nevasa	56	3704	7361	11065	44360	55425
1968	Nevasa/ Uganda	41	3330	7161	10491	38268	48759
1969	Nevasa/ Uganda	41	3494	6963	10457	39154	49611
1970	Nevasa/ Uganda	41	3129	7717	10846	35790	46636
1971	Nevasa/ Uganda	46	2932	8642	11574	41608	53182
		449	27716	62460	90176	348637	438813
1972 (estimated)	Nevasa/ Uganda	47	3000	8700	11700	40000	51700
1973 (estimated)	Nevasa/ Uganda	49	3400	8300	11700	44000	55700

By 1965 many Local Education Authorities were undertaking block-bookings of all, or part of, the dormitory accommodation for their own schools. Some Local Education Authorities, including Hampshire, Renfrewshire and Surrey, booked each year, others booked every other year. The prejudice against termtime travel, widely experienced earlier, was being overcome and techniques were adopted to occupy the ships in the more difficult periods in the school year, during examination times and the winter months. The long and tiring journeys by rail for winter cruises from Venice and Genoa were replaced by air transfer in 1965. Support from overseas countries was growing, namely from France, Germany, Canada, Sweden, Japan, their students travelling with British boys and girls. In 1964 four or five junior cruises in April and May for children aged between ten and twelve became a feature of the programme.

The sale of cabin accommodation to members of the general public was important. While occupying separate quarters they were prepared to share a cruise with over 800 school-children and enjoyed doing so. This added to the overall revenue and it played an important part in attracting the interest of associations such as The National Trust for Scotland, the Civil Defence Association and Catholic Societies, who sponsored adult cruises in which adult passengers not only occupied the cabins but also the dormitory accommodation. The National Trust for Scotland has travelled each year on this basis since 1961.

'NEVASA' AND 'UGANDA'

In 1965 the new *Nevasa* re-enters the story. Her trooping contract had been prematurely terminated at the end of 1962 and she spent more than a year laid up before a decision was made to convert her for educational cruises to replace *Dunera*. The comprehensive work, costing more than £900,000, was carried out by Silley Cox & Co. at Falmouth and this magnificent modern school ship of 21,000 tons, fitted for 307 cabin passengers and 1,090 students, joined the programme in October 1965. It was decided to retain *Dunera* for further service and in 1966 the three school ships carried nearly 54,000 passengers. This increased to over 55,600 passengers in 1967, but the introduction of new International Regulations led to the withdrawal and disposal of *Dunera* and *Devonia* at the end of the year after their long useful careers. B.I. met this unexpected development by the withdrawal of the passenger liner S.S. *Uganda* (17,000 tons) from the Company's East African and South African Service for conversion in Hamburg as a school ship for 307 cabin passengers and 920 students at a cost of nearly £3 million. She joined *Nevasa* early in 1968. Together these two school ships now undertake a programme of forty to forty-four educational cruises each year.

It would be less than honest to suggest that at every stage of development it has been possible to provide the ideal conditions for a school at sea. Remarkable adaptations have been achieved. B.I. has faced the same challenge as school architects but with different constraints; the need to meet a changing philosophy of education.

CONVERSION TO SCHOOL SHIPS

The history of the school ships from *Dunera* to *Uganda* was frequently structural. There was never as much space as one would have liked and as ideas progressed it was not always possible to introduce new developments because an essential steel bulkhead or an indispensable derrick was an obstruction!

The residential accommodation on the *Dunera* was easily adapted to the needs of school-children but, at the same time, the existing rooms imposed a design which might not have been proposed in planning a purpose-built ship. In the initial stages economics suggested that it was unwise to pour money too lavishly into a scheme until it had proved itself and gained the support of Education Authorities.

In addition to the residential side the school day had to be catered for. An Assembly Hall holding 300 people was built, classrooms installed and provision made for indoor and outdoor recreation. Because of the capacity of the Assembly Hall and classrooms, the basic organisation had to revolve round the division of the 834 children into three main groups; while one group was in the Assembly Hall, another was assigned to classrooms and the third divided between deck games and private study. This pattern remains the basis of the organisation to the present day. For the student it gives a variety of activities, but it imposes considerable strain on lecturers who have to speak three times a day. The acoustics in all four ships have been given careful attention, but it is no easy matter to make oneself heard above the noise of forced-air ventilation and other sounds inevitable when a ship is at sea!

The bold step of purchasing the Bibby Line *Devonshire*, and carrying out a second conversion, allowed some of the inadequacies discovered in 1961 to be avoided. The new *Devonia* Assembly Hall had its seats gently tiered and its axis diagonally across the ship to provide better vision of the screen but it was still only one deck high. Some flexibility was achieved in the classrooms by the use of movable screens but by and large the arrangements were similar to those in *Dunera*. After a few years' operation it was clear that one or two improvements were essential if a third ship was ever contemplated; the provision of a quiet room to which students could go who wanted to escape the pressures of a constricted life on board, and a suitable place for the display of maps and other pictorial material to give point to a cruise. There was also a serious lack of sheltered deck space where children could move around in bad weather. When the conversion of the *Nevasa* had almost been completed it was disappointing to find that although a Quiet Room had been provided and so labelled, it was immediately below the Common Room and hence a misnomer! At the same time there was no sign of a Map and Information Room and it was only after some last-minute private negotiation with the Supply Department that an intended store was surrendered and made into a room for display purposes. As for covered deck space, there was even less in the students' area than in the earlier ships. However, the Games Room was much more accessible than the submarine spaces of *Dunera* and *Devonia* and, with some ingenuity, could be used for limited physical activity. It also proved useful as a place for a 'Senior Club' for older students in the evening.

When the *Uganda* was converted into a school ship in 1967 an area of covered deck was provided and the dormitories were better sited. Although the principle of a study room equipped as a library with display facilities and comfortable seating in a quiet part of the ship was again accepted, and the final result was well furnished, the room was minute; display facilities were negligible and shelving was inadequate. It became necessary to use a neighbouring classroom for display. With a full ship this could not always be spared for the purpose.

The policy of having cabin passengers continued to provide essential revenue and to give maturity to the ethos on board. If people were to pay cabin fares, however modest, they expected facilities. Space to improve the school could not always be provided. Rarely had the art of compromise been so delicately exercised. Given these limitations, spacial and financial, educational progress had to be achieved in other directions.

The enterprise owed much to the first Director of Education in *Dunera* and to the Commander who, having seen the first school ship through her initial year, returned to command the *Devonia* in 1963. It took a long time to eradicate what has been described as 'the troop-ship mentality'. The sailors suddenly found themselves, without any possibility of retraining, in an entirely novel situation, and it is not surprising that there was some difference between their approach and that of the Headmaster of the school on board. Through the wisdom of Commodore Rogers a reasonable compromise was reached.

THE PATTERN OF EDUCATIONAL CRUISES

Today educational cruises for young people include:

Local Education Authority Cruises organised by a single L.E.A. or two or three Authorities with independent or combined programmes. Some cater for a wide age-range and others, such as Junior Cruises, for nine- to thirteen-year-olds.

Charter Cruises for educational trusts like the Scottish Secondary Schools Travel Trust.

Junior Cruises intended for younger children from individual schools or assembled by organisations such as the Incorporated Association of Preparatory Schools.

Sixth Form Cruises arranged by B.I. such as the Sixth Form Classical Cruise, or arranged by educational organisations like the General Studies Association and the Commonwealth Institute.

International Cruises on which students from overseas join with their British contemporaries. For example 2,000 Canadian students sailed with young people from different parts of the U.K. in 1971.

The preparedness of the Company to create and experiment in new fields of operation has always been a feature of its long history. In addition to providing the depth of organisation essential when a concern assumes a responsibility to thousands of children, it has been willing to meet the considerable financial burdens of originating and maintaining this project and of ensuring that the highest standards of service are provided for passengers old and young. It has brought to bear in an unusual field all the professional skills in ship operation acquired over a century because it is convinced of the benefits which these cruises provide for young passengers, not only in the academic sense but also in the important fields of community experience and international fellowship.

ADVISORY COMMITTEE FOR EDUCATIONAL CRUISES

It was decided in the early days to formalise the discussions which had been held with educationists supporting the project and an Advisory Committee met for the first time on 5 January 1962. It was composed of nominees from the Association of Education Committees, the Association of Chief Education Officers, the Association of Education Officers, the Educational Institute of Scotland, the Association of Directors of Education in Scotland, the Headmasters' Association of Scotland, Dr W. B. Inglis, Principal of Moray House College of Education, Edinburgh, and Mr E. H. Heelas, General Inspector of Schools, Birmingham.

The main business of this meeting was to assess the first year's operation in *Dunera* when 8,000 children and 2,200 adults were carried and to consider what changes of policy seemed necessary in the light of experience. Although the first year had brought a financial loss, so convinced was the B.I. Board of the potential that it was possible for the Company's Chairman to announce in his opening remarks the intention to buy what was virtually the *Dunera*'s sister ship, *Devonshire*, from the Bibby Line and to introduce her, after conversion, into the 1962 programme.

The Advisory Committee gradually increased in size as, more and more, the principal education bodies wished to be represented and it has always been the policy from time to time to invite certain interested individuals to join the official nominees. In 1972 only Messrs Cameron and Heelas remained of the original members as will be seen from the current list of members (Appendix 1).

Meetings are held once a year and members are asked to keep in touch with activities aboard by themselves taking a cruise when they are able.

4 THE SHIP'S COMPANY

*It was pretty clear from the start in 1961 that much more would be required
from the Captain on a school ship than on a troopship*
COMMODORE B. A. ROGERS

CAPTAIN, OFFICERS AND CREW

Under the regulations for transporting troops in a ship, the Captain of
the ship, his officers and crew had limited responsibility for the troops
who naturally were under the command of a military officer called the
Ship's Commandant. He was a senior officer appointed permanently to
the ship by the War Office. A ship's captain could do much to make
his ship an agreeable one in which to sail.

The Captain of a school ship has to put a lot of effort into his work
but he is greatly rewarded by the satisfaction a successful cruise gives.
Equally valuable is the real pleasure of having close personal contact
with people from the educational world, Directors of Education,
Chairmen and members of Education Committees, Government
Inspectors, Headmasters and Headmistresses and not least the Party
Leaders. Many of the cruises are organised and led by County or City
authorities and a Captain gets a very close insight into the way each
authority sets about its task. This is not achieved by a short visit to
County Hall or a school but it is by a full fortnight of close compan-
ionship in a ship and in foreign ports with all the difficulties that crop
up. All this gives the Captain a very special understanding of the
officials of the educational world. It is, of course, analogous to the
experience of the Captain of a troopship, who gained a special understanding of the Army, its regiments and their traditions and formed
friendships with many of their officers. He had an opportunity of insight into the spirit of a military unit given to very few outside the
military world, and some Captains with long service in troopers had a
knowledge of Army personnel which would have surprised the War
Office.

The ship's company in the *Nevasa* is composed of 376 officers and
ratings including a Headmaster and his two deputies, two surgeons,
two nursing sisters, seven matrons, one fire-master, five masters-at-
arms, two bank representatives and four musicians.

On the *Uganda* the ship's company comprises 366 officers, petty
officers and ratings, including the Headmaster and two deputies,
two surgeons, two nursing sisters, six matrons, bank representatives,
a fire-master, five masters-at-arms and four musicians.

In the *Nevasa* there is an Asian crew of 282 and in the *Uganda* of 268. As Commodore Rogers has said:

It was pretty clear from the start in 1961 that much more would be required from the Captain on a school ship than on a troopship. To have limited his task to keeping a clean, efficient ship steering correctly from A to B would have been to make the teachers' work more difficult and to deprive the students of useful contact with seamen. The Captain of the ship had to be involved and he and the Director of Education must work together. Each had a clear sphere of activity in which his own individual wishes and instructions were paramount, but in the more general life of the school ship it was very much a partnership. There had been precedents in other educational establishments, albeit tied to the shore – for example – the two training ships *Worcester* and *Conway*. These two ships provided pre-sea training for young cadets before going to sea.

In these ships the Captain of the ship and the Headmaster had dual control and had to work together if the ship was to be successful.

When *Dunera* started as a school ship in April 1961 it was obviously going to be important to provide something more than just a cruise, it was necessary to build up an institutional framework of staff, discipline and esprit de corps to make a happy ship and to get some of the happiness and esprit de corps passed on to the students to help make the experience formative and memorable. Experienced educationalists would have realised that this would follow, given a smart ship and efficient crew, but in 1961, to quote Commodore Rogers again: 'We could only hope and do our best.'

In a ship at sea with passengers on board the Captain has paramount authority in all cases of misbehaviour and punishment, but his powers of arrest and confinement would only be used when it was clear beyond doubt that the safety of other passengers or the ship was at risk. The steadying effect of a large number of uniformed personnel combined with the clockwork precision of a ship's routine encourages 'orderly behaviour'. Most infringements of regulations or misbehaviour are dealt with by the Headmaster or Party Leader, and only on one occasion has an offender been dismissed from the ship and flown home.

Each day routine instructions are drafted by the Headmaster after consultation with Party Leaders at the daily conference of Party Leaders and ship's officers. The movements of the ship, times of entering and leaving port, passing places of interest, etc. are dovetailed into the day's programme after consultation with the Captain.

RECOLLECTIONS OF COMMODORE B. A. ROGERS

The following recollections by Commodore Rogers show how central a role the Captain and officers play in life on board:

The final day of the cruise was always packed to bursting point with activity for the Captain – or the Staff Commander if the weather was bad. During the forenoon there would be a full inspection of the dormitories and the choice made of the best kept. At midday there was the final Party Leaders' conference to attend, followed by a pre-lunch thank-you party for them. The afternoon, after the sacrosanct siesta, brought the prize-giving ceremony, an important function rounding off the cruise and requiring a speech from the Captain with, as deserved, ingredients of praise or blame. The evening was fully occupied and required the Captain's presence at the cruise concert.

The detailed educational work and programme is of course the concern of the professional teachers. The concern of the Captain is that the ship is used in every way possible to promote and support the educational effort – to see that the students are as comfortable as it is possible to make them in a ship at sea; to see that they are well fed; and to see that the best possible educational use is made of the ship herself. A pleasant aspect is the enthusiasm of the ship's staff for their task. They work long hours but are delighted to help the students in any way possible. They capture in some way a little of that essence of devotion so typical of the good teacher.

It is often difficult for the Captain to become well known to most of the student body. In a school ship the students are on board for only a fortnight, and fog or bad weather for a few days can mean almost total isolation for the Captain. He must, however, endeavour to project his personality in order to give students a focus for their thoughts, impressions, and loyalties. If they feel that the Captain is genuinely interested they will respond unconsciously. In the event of an emergency arising this feeling of confidence will be most important. The Captain has the great advantage of wearing a distinctive uniform so that his presence at any function is immediately evident. Rounds of inspection during the forenoon attract attention. His voice over the public address system becomes recognised. Commentaries on passing places of interest, if made by the Captain, help to get his voice recognised.

Handling the ship in difficult situations helps to raise the Captain's prestige! On one occasion, arriving off the entrance to Grand Harbour in Malta and finding entry impossible owing to a north-east gale blowing, the ship was taken round to the lee of the south side of the island for several hours. Later we returned to the Grand Harbour entrance and waited for permission to enter. There was a heavy swell running into the entrance and heavy seas cascading over the breakwaters. It was not safe for the pilot boat to come out with the pilot but the harbour authorities signalled that the ship could enter if the Captain was willing to bring her in and embark his pilot inside. 'We are going in now', went out over the public address system and was greeted by a cheer from around the decks. As 21,000 tons of ship lifts to the swell and slowly closes towards the narrow entrance between the breakwaters, concentration, steadiness and deft handling of helm and engines are required. It looks very narrow from a seventy feet high bridge. It must be a slow manoeuvre because in the Grand Harbour there is a turn to port inside. Go hard at it and you would dent the fortress of Malta. Go too slow and wind and sea would push the ship to leeward and you would end up with the breakwater lighthouse taking the stage in the Assembly Hall. After neatly swinging into Bighi Bay and calmer water, we embarked the pilot safely and the ship manoeuvred alongside to let a delighted crowd of passengers get away ashore.

Here is another episode to illustrate how a Captain can procure a feather for his cap. One day in December 1961 *Dunera* was hove-to in a north-westerly gale in the Gulf of Lyons. We were to have made a visit to Ajaccio in Corsica. All day we laboured into a heavy sea. It was decided that we should have to omit Ajaccio and push on to Genoa. At two in the morning I woke up with a start and realised the wind had suddenly dropped and the motion of the ship eased. The Mediterranean had decided to clear the weather up and few seas in the world can do it so quickly. I knew my Mediterranean and trusted her as much as I mistrusted the Atlantic. I grabbed the voicepipe connecting me to the bridge and ordered the officer of the watch to alter course for Ajaccio. When the passengers came on deck in the morning the high snow-covered hills of Corsica were gleaming in the sunshine ahead. Breakfast was a cheerful meal and although we were a few hours late in arriving everybody was delighted.

EDUCATION STAFF

The Company has never expected to provide more than opportunities and facilities for the teachers to make the most of educational cruises in the interests of their students although some educationalists would now wish to see B.I. providing a more structured curriculum for students based on their unique experience in this field. The small permanent education staff appointed to the pioneer ships consisted of a Director and a Deputy Director of Education. Later, a Director and two Deputies, one being a woman, were appointed to the larger ships. The first Director of Education (initially designated Director of Studies) was a teacher who had spent most of his career since the war as an army staff officer. He was appointed to the *Dunera* a short time before she sailed on her first cruise. Tam Dalyell, now M.P. for West Lothian, at that time teaching at Bo'ness Academy, was appointed as Deputy Director until he left to nurse his constituency. He was author of the book *The Case for Ship Schools* (Civic Press, Glasgow), 1960.[1]

The introduction of *Devonia* involved two similar appointments. Relief arrangements were haphazard and the lack of an educationalist at the London Head Office caused some frustrations for the education staffs on board. One illustration of this was connected with the supply of documentary films to supplement the lectures. For the first visit to the island of Rhodes a film with the apt title *Land of Rhodes* was put on board. Fortunately the Director of Education was able to snatch a

1 Tam Dalyell is also author of *Ship School*, Newman Neame 1963.

moment for a preview, only to see an excellent but hardly relevant survey of Rhodesia.

In the early days the majority of established teachers quite naturally viewed such appointments with some wariness but, as the scheme became 'reputable' and the enforced break from orthodoxy seemed no bar to resuming a career ashore, the field of new applicants became much wider. Furthermore, it was soon realised that, as the majority of children travelling were girls, the education staff would benefit from being open to women, while the introduction of bigger ships and the increasing sophistication of the whole exercise demanded a larger permanent staff. Each ship now has an establishment of a Director and two Deputies, with provision made for relief.

Eventually, it was also appreciated that there was need for a senior educationist at Head Office to coordinate educational policy and oversee the activities of his colleagues at sea; in 1967 the post of Senior Director of Education was established to replace the haphazard presence at the office of ship's staff not on leave or at sea.

Nomenclature for the education staff has always presented problems: they began as Director and Deputy Director of Studies but the nature of their duties, so much in the early days biased towards administration, made this inappropriate, particularly when they had no power to direct the classroom side of study. They have now been renamed Headmaster and Deputy Head, but whatever the title of the office the duties are the same. With the establishment of routines and patterns the administrative problems may have become less complicated but their diversity has not become less. As the exercise has become more extensive, it has increased the need for qualities of resilience, and for physical and mental energy.

The Headmaster of the school on board is in the peculiar position of having a new school once a fortnight, with only a small staff of his own to administer it: the accompanying teachers are temporarily under his direction but he can do little directing and must achieve his objectives by advice and cajolery. Apart from his deputies, he has only two other permanent members of staff to run the complex organisation on board. These are a clerical purser in charge of the School Office and a purserette as stenographer. Much of the routine work in the School Office is undertaken by temporary staff, young men, usually between school and university, who travel as the Company's guests in return for certain duties. Their assistance is invaluable and it is hoped that what they gain from the experience in terms of seeing the world and human relationships repays the very real effort they put into their work.

Apart from the combination of tact and drive required to start the school wheels turning and to keep them suitably oiled for the duration of the cruise, the Headmaster and his Deputies require the social acumen to mix informally not only with Party Leaders but also with the cabin passengers who may or may not have any connection with education. This is an exercise in public relations which, on top of their administrative and lecturing commitments, can impose considerable mental and physical strain fortnight after fortnight through the year.

On an 'open' cruise, when schools from all over the country come together *ad hoc*, the Headmaster's task is more difficult than on cruises when all the dormitory accommodation has been booked by one or several L.E.A.s. Not only will the preparation of the students be diverse but the first verbal briefing from an expert will be given only after embarkation. The welding together of the team is therefore likely to take longer, but in these circumstances it is often remarkable what can be achieved.

If, on the other hand, it is possible for the Party Leaders to be briefed in advance and to have the opportunity to ask questions, this settling down period is much shorter and the sense of cohesion more quickly acquired. This is one of the advantages of the charter or block-booking on which one L.E.A. reserves all the dormitory accommodation or possibly a few L.E.A.s share (see Chapter 5). It is then the custom to agree in advance with the Authority or Authorities the general timetable for the cruise; to discuss certain principles, such as the attitude to smoking, and for the Senior Director of Education, or the Headmaster in charge of the cruises concerned, to brief the Party Leaders ashore about their duties and the whole organisation on board.

Whether or not it has been possible for Party Leaders to be briefed by the education staff ashore it is vital that they meet at frequent intervals during the cruise. It is not always realised that if the Party Leaders are under pressure, the ship is more so, and although the idea of consulting Party Leaders about the daily programme before it is published may have an appeal, it is just not practicable. Party Leaders' conferences are inevitably concerned with underlining and supplementing points in an already published programme – this is particularly important before a port of call – and in discussing any other immediate problems which may have arisen. There are sixty or seventy Party Leaders at these meetings and to keep them reasonably short it is essential that they are carefully chaired. This makes it all the more important that the education staff are available to Party Leaders informally, because it is to them they will take their problems whether they are of a strictly educational nature or not.

The Headmaster finds himself with a large temporary staff of teachers who may or may not be headed by a 'cruise leader', an additional temporary staff of Chaplains (Protestant, Roman Catholic and, when possible, Free Church), and usually two senior students from a college of education to assist in supervising the girls' P.E. and games, a valuable part of teacher training for the young women concerned.

Delegation is essential and the Headmaster usually allocates specific duties to his Deputies; the preparation of the Party Leaders' duty roster, coordination of voluntary activities, supervision of ship's prefects, control of visits to the ship's departments and working out the phases for shore excursions among them.

Even before he has been able to compose his report on one cruise he is embroiled in the details of the next, since the turn-round time is minimal.

Although the education staff are concerned primarily with administration, considerable advances have been made in educational cruises by extending the subjects covered by lectures and providing facilities for additional study. As the education staff increased and the administrative burden was thereby lightened – and by the gradual establishment of expertise and routine – other improvements were possible. The employment of subject specialists ensured that additional background lectures could be given either as part of the compulsory timetable or to a voluntary audience.

If the ship is sailing close to any interesting landmark, a commentary from the bridge provides a valuable supplement to the content of the cruise. Such commentaries were, for a time, given by the Captain but they have become increasingly a part of the education staff's responsibility. Favourite subjects are Gibraltar, Navarino Bay, the passage of the Sound between Denmark and Sweden, and some of the sites of historic naval actions off the Atlantic coast of Europe. During a cruise including Famagusta, Malta and Ephesus it is possible to go close to Rhodes and Lindos and give commentaries on the themes of the Knights of St John and the Journeys of St Paul.

MATRON AND MEDICAL DEPARTMENT

When educational cruising was launched in 1961 a new department within the make-up of a ship's manning was instituted – the School Matron's Department – and with it the final touch to the boarding school at sea.

For the teacher who has perhaps less experience of school visits abroad, B.I. cruises are a valuable introduction in the sense that they are relieved of some of the burden of pastoral care for twenty-four hours of the day; this is one of the big differences between the B.I. venture and the position of a teacher who takes a party on the Continent on his own.

What difficulties did those pioneering Matrons of 1961 and 1962 encounter in this new school world? They had to adjust themselves to living and working in a man's world, and at the same time these Matrons, whose past experience had been in boarding schools ashore, found themselves dealing with children who, in many cases, had never been away from home before. Dormitories and community life were foreign to them, as well as to their Party Leaders. British India's first Senior Matron recalls these cruises.

Diplomacy was the keynote in establishing good team-work with the educational and ship's staff. Officers and men Party Leaders never failed to respond to: 'Mr So-and-So, I wonder if you can help me.' From the first I made it clear to my staff, and this has been passed on by succeeding Matrons, that the main thing to remember was that we were entrusted with the care of other people's children, and we had to endeavour to take the place of 'Mother' for a fortnight.

I can recall on my first visit to Leningrad being asked by a rather imposing Russian woman 'What are you'? I replied, 'I am the Mother of all these children.' With a look of incredulity on her face, and obviously determined not to be outdone, she said 'I am the Grand-Mamma of Leningrad!' Some Grand-Mamma, for she turned out to be the Chief of Port Police!

What do the School Matrons do? Their duties are twofold. Being a uniformed member of the ship's company, the Matron is responsible to the Captain for the general welfare of the students travelling in dormitory accommodation, with particular emphasis on the care of the girls. As such, in line with other uniformed members, she is responsible for the safety of the students and the safety of the ship. The Matron and her staff of assistant matrons play an important part in the Emergency Drill, and each assistant matron is responsible for clearing dormitory sections when the alarm goes, and for being with the students at their muster stations, helping them to put on life jackets and assisting the Party Leaders in keeping them quiet and orderly. All newly joined women officers, including the matrons, undergo a special fire-fighting course in Liverpool. Matrons do deck patrols, particularly when the ship is entering and leaving port, and this applies especially when the students first embark, seeing that they keep their feet on the deck: boys do like to climb and the ship's rails are very inviting!

On the Matron's shoulders rests responsibility for liaison with the Purser and Second Steward in connection with the domestic side of the dormitories; linen changes during the cruise, mending towels and bedcovers; keeping stores and all the rest of this important 'family' work.

The school side of a Matron's duties is important, for she and her staff must work closely with the Headmaster and Party Leaders over the various problems that inevitably arise when a large number of children are gathered together within the confines of a ship. Adaptability to the needs of the various age groups is essential, and when primary schools travel additional staff and Party Leaders are required for these young children who need extra care and supervision both in dormitories and on shore. She may be called upon to comfort the boy of thirteen who arrives at the Duty Room clutching a letter from his home telling him his puppy has died, or to break, with the Party Leader, the news, that his mother has had a serious accident.

But some of the most unnerving experiences are also the funniest. The story is told how,

On the *Devonia* when we had a Force 12 gale – in the Bay of Biscay we caught the end of Hurricane Hilda and we hove-to. The ship had stopped, we couldn't move for a day and a half, and the ship rolled, everything smashed and everybody was seasick. Whilst this was going on, the Matron was going around keeping up morale, and there wedged under one of the seats on board . . . on the deck, was a little boy who was writing a postcard and it was one of those lovely postcards of cruising ships, a beautiful white ship, blue sea, blue sky, and she helped him up and she took the postcard and written on it was – 'Dear Mum, Wish you were here instead of me.'

The adaptability of the Matrons was put to a test when the Company during slack school periods in September started adult cruising and this meant adults in the dormitories. The same Matron recalls: 'An Irish adult cruise to Rome in 1962 was our initiation into this new world. Ages from eighteen to eighty years in dormitories – the first muster stations: "You tell the dear Captain we'll go down with the ship. We can't walk up those stairs." '

Parents will no doubt ask themselves what happens in times of sea-sickness or when Mary or John is ill? In rough weather when there is mass sea-sickness, the assistant matrons are always around in the cafeteria trying to tempt the students to take some light food, for being sick on an empty stomach plays havoc with morale, and hinders recovery. Beef tea or Bovril, biscuits and rolls are made available by the Catering Purser on these occasions, and the serving of this is undertaken by the Matron's department. Sea-sickness has a short life. Within twenty-four hours the main body of students have recovered, and the Catering Purser and Chef find that appetites return and second helpings are the order of the day.

The Matron has a duty room easily visited by both boys and girls, and it is to this room that students come, ostensibly on medical grounds but often for home-sickness or home problems. A record of advance notifications of students' ailments is held here, so that a watch can be kept on these students during the night and day. The duty room is manned twenty-four hours a day; the assistant matrons patrol the girls' dormitories regularly throughout the night, and the Masters-at-Arms the boys' dormitories. Any sick child is first dealt with in the duty room and if necessary taken to hospital.

Adjacent to the dormitories, and under supervision from the Matron's duty room, are the girls' hair-drying room and the launderettes, where the students can wash their clothes.

There are separate launderettes for boys and girls. Experience proved that in a communal room the girls came off worse because they invariably did the boys' washing for them. Imagination does not have to stretch far to realise that supervision is essential in the launderettes. Night assistant matrons keep an eye on the drying-rooms, take out the dry clothing and fold it up so that the children can collect it next day. In spite of this it is surprising how much lost property is collected at the end of a cruise and unfortunate that half the children don't know what clothes they have lost.

The dormitories are arranged in sections throughout the ship, and the berthing is so organised that the girls are quite separate from the boys. Each student has his or her own bunk and locker, and they are taught to keep their dormitories tidy. At the end of each cruise the Captain gives a prize for the best kept boys' and girls' dormitory. The Party Leaders, together with the Matrons, Staff Officer and Masters-at-Arms are responsible for supervision in the dormitories, both in the morning and when the students go to bed.

The Matron's department deals with day-to-day welfare and minor ailments, but it is on the Medical Department the ultimate health of the students depends. It is manned by two surgeons and two nursing sisters, with two wards, one for boys and one for girls, a side ward, surgery and dispensary. There are two surgeries a day, one at 8.30 a.m. and the other at 4.30 p.m., and emergencies are seen and dealt with at any time. The first surgery of the cruise sees all the students who have brought doctors' letters or medicines. If any student is admitted to hospital parents can rest assured that, in addition to the specialised treatment given, the nursing staff see to it that the patients are kept happy and occupied with suitable recreational activities, books, jig-saw puzzles, etc. In some cases, where they are well enough to be up but cannot go ashore, one of the ship's boats is put down and the students are taken for a trip round the harbour where the ship is berthed.

Although the hospital is equipped to deal with surgical cases it may become necessary in some instances for the patient to be put ashore, and this is done quickly and efficiently.

There is always a doctor and sister on call in the hospital. In addition to the care of the students they are responsible for the health of the cabin passengers and ship's company, so their practice is large and at times a very hard and busy one.

CHAPLAINS

Chaplains are appointed for each cruise. A Methodist chaplain, on a Local Education Authority cruise in 1970 wrote afterwards:

Preparation began a full year before the actual cruise, and by the turn of the year the chaplains representing the Anglican, Roman Catholic and Free Churches had been selected. None of us had ever done this sort of work before, and we knew only in the most general sense what our duties would be. We knew that there would be over 900 students and nearly a hundred teachers and L.E.A. staff, in addition to independent cabin passengers and crew on board, and we were asked to consider ourselves chaplains to all groups. The chaplains met on three occasions before the cruise but found it difficult to make any precise preparations. As it turned out this was not a bad thing for we brought no preconceived plan of action into a situation of life on board ship of which we were previously ignorant.

From those in authority we received every help, courtesy and encouragement. Although individually the chaplains had to make their own position and place on the cruise, it was apparently taken for granted among the Party Leaders that there was a rightful place for us to occupy. We were invited to be at every Party Leaders' conference before and during the cruise and were invited to make contributions and express opinions quite freely.

A school assembly was held every morning that the ship was at sea and we developed our own system of carrying this out. Though we began by all three taking part during the quarter of an hour allotted it became obvious after the first of the assemblies that this was not the best way, and after that two of the chaplains contributed each morning, one leading the assembly and the other giving a short talk, linking biblical accounts and church history with the cruise and topical issues. Cabin passengers as well as students were invited to these assemblies and the number of adults and students attending on a voluntary basis was quite encouraging. The Mass was said each morning by the Roman Catholic chaplain and the Anglican and Free Church chaplains celebrated Holy Communion most mornings, one assisting the other according to whether the Anglican or Methodist form was used. In addition Mass or Holy Communion was held later in the day on occasion to cater for older people among the cabin passengers. The attendance at Communion generally was very good and the services apparently played an important part in the life of the ship. There was only one Sunday involved, midway through the cruise, and despite the fact that it had been a long tiring day in visiting Ephesus there was a huge crowd present at the Captain's service at 9 p.m. All three chaplains took part, together with the Captain and a student who read the lessons.

Both assemblies and the Captain's service were very much helped by the Director of Music who formed an orchestra and choir, trained them relentlessly, and used the results of his training to great effect.

Apart from the formal occasions, much of the chaplains' work was in the more demanding aspect of mingling with the passengers on decks, in the smoking room and music room, in dancing and leisure activities, visiting the Hospital and the dormitories at the end of the day. It was noticeable that after the first week at sea relations became much less formal and it was in this situation that the most creative work of all was done.

There are many moving experiences in which the chaplains have been involved. Perhaps one of the most rare was when the ship's Anglican chaplain, a former Bishop of Southampton, a frequent terminal port – baptised a student, using the upturned ship's bell as a font, while the *Uganda* was moored at the Israeli port of Haifa. The student had asked to be baptised in the River Jordan but the precise timing for shore visits was against this. The ceremony took place as near as possible, on board ship, with christening presents from the Captain and the Bishop and a cake provided by the Chief Steward in honour of the occasion.

5 PLANNING A CRUISE – ORGANISATION

These preparations seem to have paid off
A COUNTY EDUCATION OFFICER

LOCAL EDUCATION AUTHORITY CRUISES

Although individual schools and individual students book places on a cruise, the dormitory accommodation on most cruises is booked by Local Education Authorities, either singly or as a group of two or three. Nearly half the L.E.A.s in Great Britain book accommodation for a fortnight each year or eighteen months and encourage schools to take part. At least one Authority aims to encourage every secondary school leaver who wants to do so to take part; cruises are one aspect of residential experience which this Authority recommends for all secondary pupils.

In cases of real hardship, some Authorities make grants towards the fare, but normally pupils pay the cost without subsidy. Many of them work in the holidays to raise the money and this in itself is valuable. Some Authorities pay the fare money into a fund as it is collected and, from the interest on the fund they are able to help the parent who has paid the deposit but for genuine reasons finds it impossible to meet the whole cost. In some areas this is achieved through the formation of a Cruise Committee which is then registered as a trust benefiting from tax relief on the interest from the advance payments made by the students. The Committee is drawn from staff in the Education Office and teachers some of whom will be heads. A deposit of £5 is collected from the students and weekly payments of £1.60 over a period. Details of the form of agreement to meet this are given in Appendix 2.

The growth of school visits, including residential experience both at home and abroad, may point to the need to review the function of B.I. educational cruises within the total pattern of educational visits, a suggestion discussed in Chapter 9.

Some L.E.A.s find that other opportunities for overseas travel and exchange affect the demand for places but in most areas there is no difficulty in allocating the accommodation or in filling unexpected vacancies.

If the cruise is booked by an L.E.A., much of the administrative work leading up to the departure is done by a member of staff in the Education Department. Some Party Leaders may prefer to go with their school on their own but there are many advantages in being part of a larger organisation. The school is relieved of some administrative work and the problems and changes of arrangements which occur during the preparation period can be dealt with through the L.E.A. Another advantage of mounting a Local Education Authority Cruise is that it helps to make 'the Office' less remote. Administrative staff who have little chance of meeting teachers do so regularly in the planning period, and they have an unusual opportunity for social contact on board. It is a chance for members of the Committee and Chief Education Officers to be in direct touch with children instead of always seeing them on paper as, 'four-form entries', 'units for the calculation of teachers' salaries' or 'pupil/teacher ratios'. These have a new meaning when the Chief Education Officer tries to comfort a small boy suffering, over the taffrail, from the motion of the Bay of Biscay and is told – 'Don't mind me, Sir, it's all part of the experience.'

There are advantages too in connection with pre-cruise preparation. The school library and museum services are more easily mobilised and the Authority's advisers are available. School parties may be grouped together on a district basis and under a leader work to a syllabus. The teachers who are to be Party Leaders meet at intervals, exchange ideas and make their specialist contribution.

A county or city cruise has the effect of bringing young people from different districts together. This not only means they widen their circle but helps them to feel part of the larger community to which they belong. For the first time in the student's life he may realise he is part of his county or city, especially if by arrangement with the Captain, the county or city standard is flown during the cruise.

In the preparation period for an L.E.A. cruise, the community becomes more involved as time goes on. Most schools organise meetings of parents to discuss the itinerary. These are popular meetings, often illustrated by slides and films made on previous cruises as well as by the films on free loan from B.I. The local press is usually interested in school affairs and is likely to follow the progress of the cruise. Some papers pay for telephone calls to the ship at sea to get copy and to keep the district in touch during the cruise. Others send a reporter on board. Television and radio, particularly local radio, have produced full length programmes on L.E.A. cruises. On occasions teachers have played an active part in these programmes, arranged material and, after training through the B.B.C., acted as interviewers. This interest does not end with the cruise; on the return there is a demand for speakers from the staff of the L.E.A. and the schools to address Women's Institutes and similar gatherings. Again, this helps to bring people into touch with modern developments in education.

To give one example from many, at the end of the cruise one city Education Authority staged a large-scale exhibition for the public in the City Art Gallery to which each participating school was invited to contribute mounted displays of work done before, during and after the cruise, and a film was made for the Authority by one of their advisers, for the use of schools in the area.

In some cases, the L.E.A. will set up a joint working party of teachers and officers to assess the value of the cruise and their report may be based on an analysis of replies to detailed questionnaires completed by Party Leaders on their return.

Another advantage of a Local Education Authority cruise is that since a fair number of students go on more than one cruise during their school life, the L.E.A. can work towards an integrated programme of cruises involving the Eastern and Western Mediterranean, the Baltic Sea and Russia and the Atlantic. In this way a student may, during his seven years of secondary school life, visit countries and remote places and gain experience and understanding of the world which could hardly be acquired more effectively.

THE PLANNING SCHEDULE

The following timetable for one Authority cruise in June 1970 gives an idea of the planning and administration required.

8 January 1969	Dates agreed with B.I. Itinerary discussed over next few months.
27 June 1969	Itinerary settled. Costs agreed.
1 July 1969	Insurance covers arranged.
20 August 1969	First letter to head teachers giving details of dates, costs, etc. and asking for numbers of pupils interested.
11 September 1969	Discussions with Medical Officer of Health about medical examinations, vaccinations, etc.
14 October 1969	Second letter to head teachers allocating places, asking for students' names and deposits, and distributing B.I. Cruise Brochure, 'Information for Party Leaders', etc.
8 November 1969	Deposits received. (The major headache now is to ensure that we end up with 920 pupils with the correct boy/girl ratio. This is the single most difficult task compounded of mathematics, guesswork and sheer blind luck!)
21 November 1969	Official booking details sent to schools, including information on insurance, group passports, and vaccination.
5 December 1969	First meeting with B.I. Senior Director of Education. Educational policy settled in some detail: lecture programme, discipline policy, excursion arrangements, etc.
20 December 1969	Adminstrative party settled:

    1 Cruise leader
    2 Deputy cruise leader
    3 Organiser of physical education
    4 County music organiser
    5 Organiser of home economics
    6 Principal youth officer for the county
    7 Secretary.

22 January 1970	First Party Leaders' Meeting: B.I. Senior Director of Education present.
25 January 1970	Chaplains appointed; also P.E. students from college of education.
27 January 1970	Nominal rolls to B.I.
17 March 1970	Final arrangements confirmed with schools.
27 April 1970	Six groups arranged carefully to achieve balance of ages and interests. Embarkation arrangements made.
29 April 1970	Allocation of teachers to optional activities programme.
12 May 1970	Final Party Leaders' Meeting.
29 May 1970	Duty rota of administrative staff sent to schools.
3 June 1970	Departure. 917 students!
19 June to 1 September 1970	Aftermath: insurance payments, refunds, reports, etc.

This brief account of the arrangements by one Local Education Authority does less than justice to all its detailed planning to ensure that schools and parents are well informed, to establish the right atmosphere in terms of team spirit and rapport with the ship's company, and to achieve high educational standards.

DOCUMENTATION AND BERTHING FOR SCHOOL PARTIES

It requires little imagination to appreciate the administration which, parallel with the work in the L.E.A. office, devolves on B.I. head-quarters. As soon as a firm booking is received from an Authority or school, nominal rolls are sent with confirming letters. When these have been completed and returned to Head Office, a dormitory berthing book is compiled for each cruise. What may appear to be a fairly simple operation in berthing up to 1090 students in 1090 dormitory berths is an extremely complex undertaking, akin to a foot-ball pool permutation. For obvious if unpopular reasons boy and girl students may not share the same dormitory, or even the same section, so that there has to be a good deal of juggling to balance the sexes. As dormitories, fifty on *Nevasa* and forty-three on *Uganda*, vary in size from twelve to forty-two berths and are grouped in twelve sections on *Nevasa* and five on *Uganda*, the addition or cancellation of one student may necessitate a complete revision of the berthing. A balance also has to be made in individual dormitories according to the age of students.

In 1971 the B.I. ships carried 17,538 boy and 20,698 girl students including 1145 Canadians, 126 French students and 158 American and German students from West Germany. That there was not one single berthing error redounds to the credit of B.I. organisation.

When air movements are involved a further complication arises. Students in dormitories on the starboard side of the ship embark and disembark on the first day of the movement, and students in port side dormitories on the second day.

When dormitory berthing is almost finalised, schools are sent blank manifest pages to complete. On return, these separate sheets are compiled into a master manifest which contains a list of names and addresses, required by mercantile law, passport number, expiry date, place of issue and date of birth. For administrative purposes a note of dormitories allocated to schools is also produced. In addition, when an air movement is involved flight manifests are required.

PATTERN OF ORGANISATION

Since 1961 there have been charters, block bookings, part block bookings or individual school bookings from 209 L.E.A.s in the U.K. A slight experience of the British educational system will suggest that, within the broad framework laid down by B.I., there will be an infinite variety of views and practice on the educational purpose, planning and organisation.

Some L.E.A.s restrict the selection of students to particular age groups, or lay greater emphasis on certain age groups. For example, they see this as offering special opportunities to children in the middle years of schooling (8–12 or 9–13); opportunities which can be closely related to enquiry based activities in school and afterwards; others believe it provides an admirable context for sixth form study; others consider there should be no barrier to selection, not even the exigencies of the G.C.E., and it is not unknown for some students to sit an 'O' or 'A' level paper on board. After discussion with B.I., one or two L.E.A.s have based their charter cruise on a specialised theme, for example the study of volcanic activity described in Chapter 6, 'Planning the Curriculum'. To work on these independent lines may pose organisational problems for British India in terms of their overall programme and navigational requirements; it also demands a great deal of thought and planning on the part of the L.E.A. and its advisers.

It might be invidious to suggest that some cruises are more successful than others; to substantiate the reasons it would be necessary to mount a major piece of educational research. It is, however, an interesting reflection that many of the most successful cruises are with younger children and with sixth formers. Possibly the factors which contribute to a successful cruise are identical with those which create a 'good school', the most important being the selection and preparation of Party Leaders because, however meticulous the administration both of B.I. and the Local Education Authority's headquarters staff, everything depends, at the end of the day, on the patience, skill and enthusiasm of the Party Leaders. They may be relieved of some problems by the ship's staff and the presence on board of the Chief Education Officer but theirs is an intimate and personal responsibility to the anxious, excited, forgetful, or obstreperous individuals in their group.

Table 2

1961–1971

	(a) total number of counties	(b) number of counties from which schools have travelled	(c) number of counties who have chartered, blockbooked or part block- booked accommoda- tion	(d) number of authorities in column (c) from which schools have also travelled independently
England and Wales	60	60	38	33
Scotland	31	31	14	14
N. Ireland	6	6	3	3
Channel Islands	2	2	—	—
	99	99	55	50

	total number of county boroughs	number of county boroughs from which schools have travelled*	number of county boroughs who have char- tered, block- booked or part block- booked ac- commodation	number of authorities in column (c) from which schools have travelled in- dependently
England and Wales	83	71	27	23
Scotland	4	4	4	4
N. Ireland	2†	2†	—	—
	89	77	31	27
I.L.E.A. and London boroughs	21	21	11	11

* Columns (a) and (b) are identical as far as counties are concerned because schools from every county have travelled. There are twelve county boroughs from which no schools have yet travelled.
† Plus 2 boroughs from Eire.

The varied pattern of organisation adopted by L.E.A.s reflects the same debate which continues on land; is it better to have vertical grouping under the students' own teachers for pastoral care and classroom work or a combination of both, with horizontal grouping for school periods? If there is horizontal grouping should it be based on age or ability? Should the teacher with a special interest in Byzantine architecture move round the groups for 'teaching periods' or stay with his own group? Although the classroom activities as such take up a relatively small portion of the total day at sea, all the speculations about setting and banding, team teaching, 'micro and macro learning situations' are exchanged in the Party Leaders' common room or during rare moments of respite, on the sun deck.

It would be a platitude to suggest that the most effective arrangement is the one in which the L.E.A. and its schools have most confidence. A few of the advantages and disadvantages of different approaches are discussed in Chapter 7. Since a day at sea can be twice as exacting for the Party Leader as a day in school, the simplest organisation whereby the Party Leader spends as much time as possible with his own students is probably the best.

The way in which the cruise is planned not only affects what happens on board but the preparatory work in school – the more the Party Leaders are in touch with their own students the greater the continuity.

Many L.E.A.s who make block or part block bookings issue a handbook for Party Leaders and/or students which incorporates or supplements the 'Notes for the Guidance of Party Leaders at sea or in port', compiled by B.I. This might include information on: administrative and head office party, ship's personnel, itinerary, schedule of schools and accommodation, method of getting to point of embarkation, ship's prefects, typical day at sea, draft timetable, voluntary activity periods, senior club, educational games facilities and equipment, pocket money and optional tours, insurance, street plans of places to be visited, phrases in the language of the countries, background reading.

Some handbooks go beyond technical information and include information briefs and book lists also prepared by B.I., maps and students' worksheets. The County Education Officer of an Authority which took part with students from thirty-nine secondary schools in a cruise to Lisbon, Lanzarote, Madeira and Ponta Delgada in July 1971 wrote:

The essence of what we did was to organise the educational programme in discussions with teacher Party Leaders well in advance and, of course, with the necessary consultation with the ship's Director of Education. We were therefore able a long time before the cruise to provide all Party Leaders with a draft timetable which showed them what a typical day at sea was like and how each group would be occupied in lectures, classroom work, deck games, private study and voluntary activities.

We were also faced with the problem that all the educational work on the cruise ought to be concentrated on the places we visited, but that the Party Leaders might be specialised in every subject of the school curriculum without any particular knowledge of the history or geography of the area. We therefore prepared 19 information briefs, covering as many aspects as we could think of, of Lisbon and the Islands, and we issued these at intervals over the twelve months before the cruise took place to every Party Leader and every student including students on the reserve list.

Some of the briefs for this cruise which were written either by the Local Education Authority's staff or specialists in the schools ranged from food and cooking in Portugal and Spain to vulcanology, and from the sea fishing industries of the Iberian Peninsula to an introduction to navigation. An essay on the Portuguese discoverers by the County Education Officer must have provided him with welcome relief from writing Education Committee Reports!

Some of the administrative and head office staff were chosen for the help they could give on the educational side not only with music and P.E. but with history, geography and nautical education.

PARTY LEADERS

The role of the Party Leader is demanding, before and during the cruise. In addition to the administrative details and planning of students' work, there are meetings with other leaders, with students and with parents. Having this exacting role in mind, B.I. sends out in advance to Party Leaders a number of documents designed to help in making the cruise as fruitful an experience as possible and to limit the bewilderment of teachers and students travelling, often for the first time, in an entirely strange environment. 'Information for Party Leaders' outlines all the administrative procedures prior to the cruise; 'Notes for the guidance of Party Leaders', mentioned earlier, deals with life and routine on board, information, bibliographies and language sheets on the places to be visited and suggestions for study. A week or so before sailing 'Advice to Party Leaders' is despatched; it covers matters of immediate interest from 'What to expect on the day of embarkation' to 'Avoiding uncooked food ashore', and contains the ship's rules and safety regulations.

The success of a cruise depends largely on the Party Leaders and on the extent to which they have prepared themselves. One of their problems is to avoid the tendency to become too preoccupied with organisational minutiae at the expense of planning projects, methods of teaching to be adopted and the selection and collection of materials and equipment to be taken on board. But, obvious as it may seem, the more fully the Party Leader has prepared all aspects of the timetable in this way, the more rewarding will be the fortnight on board.

Within the overall policy laid down by the L.E.A. it is usual for the selection of teachers and students, the detailed arrangements in cooperation with parents, and the planning of students' work on board to be the responsibility of the individual school. Where schools book accommodation independently they are of course themselves responsible for negotiating with British India.

In choosing Party Leaders the Head tries to achieve a balance of experience and subject interest bearing in mind the needs of those pupils left behind in school. In most cases it is not necessary to employ supplementary staff; some schools restructure their timetables while a cruise party is absent, making this a feature period for social, sporting and leisure activities. Students are selected by the school within any restrictions, for instance on age range, laid down by the L.E.A. Where it has been the policy not to exclude pupils on grounds of character or discipline this has almost always been justified. One Head wrote: 'I had a lad in my party who was a great nuisance in the school and I was doubtful about bringing him, but I am glad now that I did. We have seen each other in a new light.'

One of the most important aspects of preparation is the opportunity it provides for a close link with the parents. The Party Leader who may be under mounting pressure during the final count down before departure is not always aware of the anxiety and gratitude experienced by most parents. Anxiety as in the case of one mother from the depths of rural England who said to the Party Leader on departure: 'You will look after my little girl won't you. I am afraid of all these Italian lads!' And gratitude expressed by the parents of a boy of 12 in a party from one of the Home Counties just before he embarked:

On returning home one day our son told us that his school was embarking on another educational cruise, taking a group of twelve-year-olds. Our immediate reaction was 'What a wonderful opportunity' for youngsters of his age and we hoped that he might be one of the fortunate boys selected.

Later a meeting was held at school for interested parents to see a film showing activities undertaken by the children preparing for the trip and during it, also giving an opportunity to question the group's leading teacher on such things as passports, pocket money, medical facilities, etc., and the most important – cost! After further discussion at home as to the cost and benefits to be gained from such a trip and our son's assurance that he wished without any reservation to be selected, the deposit was paid.

Our son had been selected – and it became much more of a reality when we saw all the preparation work that had to be undertaken and we realised that the venture was not being taken lightheartedly and that when embarkation hour arrived no opportunity would be missed through lack of preparation. Much of this work was done during the children's lunchtime at school, also a great deal at home; undertaking written projects and a visit to the

Planetarium, apparently proving most interesting to the boys, as a talk was given on the star formation they hope to see.

All preparation is now complete – the opportunity and benefit to be gained is in our son's hands – let us hope he has the character to take it.

CHECKLIST FOR PARTY LEADERS

The following checklist of action for Party Leaders was drawn up by a Devonshire school after long experience of educational cruising.

Provisional numbers
1 Letter to parents giving dates, route, cost and asking for return of provisional acceptance slip
2 Notify provisional numbers to County Hall

Firm numbers
3 Details of cruise to parents:
　a. Total cost
　b. Payments scheme
　c. Immediate payment of deposit
　d. Return of proforma giving
　　(i) Personal details
　　(ii) Permission for all necessary immunisations to be given by school medical officer
　　(iii) Formal permission to travel

Payments
4 Prepare receipt slips
5 Make provisional list of pupils and rule up payments record
6 Notify firm numbers to County Hall and pay deposits via school account
7 Duplicate Nominal roll
8 Open deposit a/c to earn interest on early payments

Briefing
9 Meeting with parents. For this prepare:
　a. Kit lists
　b. Precis of insurance details
　c. Ship's timetable
　Request details of special medical and dietary requirements
10 When B.I. send payments record cards, transfer to them details of previous payments and issue them

Passports
11 Decide what kind of passport is best: write to passport office or phone labour exchange
12 Arrange immunisations with school M.O.
13 Prepare B.I. nominal roll
14 Tie up arrangements for party travel to port or airport and the return journey

Final arrangements
15 Arrange for information centre at school *and after school* for use on day of return

16 Prepare and distribute
   a. Cruise folders
   b. Spare kit lists
   c. Notebooks and/or writing paper
17 Collect medicines
18 Arrange to take instruments for ship's concert
19 Make and publish firm arrangements about:
   a. Time and place for departure
   b. Time and place for return
   c. Telephone numbers of:
      (i) day information centre
      (ii) the centre to be used after 5 p.m.
   d. List of names and addresses (other than the visual ones) for notification if return arrangements have to be changed
20 KEEP FINGERS CROSSED!

6 PLANNING THE CURRICULUM

No part of the school curriculum can make its full contribution to education in isolation. . .

Schools Council Working Paper No. 38

PRE-CRUISE PREPARATION

During the past ten years teachers have been looking with fresh interest at the environment as a means of making studies more relevant. They have turned to the local environment – to the school grounds for practical mathematics or simple ecology – and to places in other parts of the country for biological and geographical field work and adventure courses. Educational Cruises offer the chance to extend this work through individual and group enquiry and to explore special interests before the cruise, on board and ashore. It will depend how the teaching strength is organised but in many Local Education Authority cruises it is possible to pool the experience and interests of teachers to achieve something like a team-teaching situation.

There are, however, practical difficulties such as the diversity of ages and interests among the groups which make up the 'passenger list' which prevents as close an integration between the illustrated lectures and bridge commentaries by the B.I. Educational Staff and the programmes of work planned by Party Leaders as some would desire. This is a problem worth further discussion when considering future developments in educational cruising.

Preparatory work will vary according to the size and ages of the groups and the abilities and interests of the members of the party. In some schools it may depend on the extent to which external examinations loom on the horizon. Today it is rare to find subject teachers who are obsessed with the fear that if a pupil misses three or four of 'their lessons' they will be doomed for the rest of their lives but some schools still prefer preparation for educational visits to take place 'out of school'. If the students are to get value from the mass of impressions and experiences they will meet during their fortnight away, and study periods on board are not to degenerate into 'money-changing sessions', preparation is essential, even if time can only be spared as part of the dinner hour once or twice a week. Some schools form a Cruise Club and invite guest speakers; someone from the B.I. staff, for example, to give a talk, supported by films, on topics like 'The Day at Sea'. Visits are arranged to the London Planetarium and parents are invited to sessions on the music, art, food, clothes and customs of the places to be visited and to the final briefing before departure. In addition to visiting speakers, and the growing practice of calling on children or parents from Cyprus, Greece and Turkey to help with the language, one idea is to invite a chef from the local Greek or Italian restaurant to provide a typical meal of his country in place of the normal school dinner!

B.I. provides book-lists, language sheets and general information, but this is frequently supplemented by material which students are encouraged to build up for themselves; a large map of Europe, or Admiralty chart on which to mark their route and give relevant statistical information on each country to be visited – data which can usually be got from an up-to-date *Whitaker's Almanack* – and posters and booklets from travel agencies or cultural organisations representing the countries concerned. To avoid a flood of individual requests descending on the desks of hard-pressed staff 'at the receiving end', some coordination is necessary when writing for material.

Most schools have sufficient notice before the cruise to plan at least fourteen sessions for a Cruise Club. If the party returns during termtime a follow-up is possible while the experience is still fresh but many teachers have found that students need time to readjust themselves before they are asked to start making reports. Post-cruise activities often include a meeting when parents and pre-cruise speakers are invited to see and discuss the students' display of work; souvenirs, art, photography and other projects. Some students are encouraged to give written or verbal reports to school societies or to lead discussion groups on topics suggested by the cruise.

The following is a cross section of ideas and material to illustrate the variety of ways in which different schools approach the planning of activities, which may help teachers preparing for a cruise for the first time. It leaves many gaps and does not presume to comment on the suggestions and experience offered.

REPORT ON A MIDDLE SCHOOL PROGRAMME BY THE PARTY LEADER

S.S. *Uganda* Cruise: Vigo, Gibraltar, Porto, La Rochelle May 1971. For us the cruise was an integral part of our Middle School programme. We look upon a project, theme or journey as a vehicle for developing certain study skills. Each project or journey will obviously carry a different content of knowledge and experience but will serve to develop the same basic tools of learning.

In determining what these skills are we have borrowed heavily from the Schools' Council Environmental Studies Project and we identify eighteen skills for the guidance of our teachers:

1 Use of reference books
2 Factual writing

3 Imaginative writing
4 Letter writing
5 Construction and use of questionnaires
6 Interviewing
7 Class/group discussion
8 Drama and movement
9 Comparing past/present/future
10 Use of documents, plans, photos

11 Mathematics
12 Experimentation
⎰ We do not attempt to cover all our maths or science through our 'Studies' but merely to make some aspects more meaningful

13 Collecting and classifying
14 Mapping
15 Weather recording
16 Modelling/needlework, etc.
17 Pictorial representation
18 Recording and displaying

Within this framework there is much freedom for the individual teacher to operate and he has the security that the work is part of a coordinated pattern. This pattern allows for the comprehensive development of the pupils. Whether a class is 'dipping' in the local pond, studying the Romans or visiting a museum the work can be directed to the common goal of skill development.

Here are some brief examples of how we keyed the S.S. *Uganda* cruise to our programme:

1 Searching for information re Oporto, Gibraltar apes, etc., and re-using the information to answer specific questions.
2 Reports of visits ashore and life on board ship.
3 Mainly in connection with the sea, dolphins, night, a sailor's life.
4 Letters of thanks after the cruise to guides in Portugal and school-children in France. Letters to tourist offices requesting literature.
5 and 6 These were developed in connection with the crew. The captain allowed himself to be interviewed.
7 Did not have to be planned for – it arose throughout the cruise and before and after.
8 Spanish dancers at Vigo inspired Spanish-type movements in our later dance-drama work. Castanets and Spanish music were used.
9 Cape Trafalgar and the cemetery at Gibraltar helped us compare life at sea in past and present eras.
10 Much use was made of photos of Gibraltar, etc. in the pre-cruise period. Plans of our ports of call were very useful as were plans of the ship layout.
11 Mathematics came through distances covered and speeds of the ship. Bridge visit gave rise to the use of polar coordinates and other navigational maths.
12 Pre-cruise work was done re flotation, displacement, streamlining

of ships, etc. The group tried many experiments connected with purifying salt water.

13 Shells were collected in Spain, France and from the Mediterranean. These were classified according to various criteria.

14 Route maps, maps of western Europe and city maps were drawn before the cruise. Much reference was made to atlases and the globe.

15 This was done in connection with the ship's weather service. Statistics were collected and recorded by the children. Beaufort wind-scale was introduced.

16 Models of the La Rochelle chain towers etc. Girls made dolls and designed Spanish costumes.

17 Paintings of the S.S. *Uganda* and of Gibraltar and sketches of interesting bridges, arches, buoys, etc. formed part of the recording.

18 Individual cruise books were compiled and an exhibition of work was mounted for parents and children.

Of course the benefits of the expedition were not confined to this business of skill development. There was all the joy and value of fresh experiences, of living together and of seeing foreign places which have been referred to elsewhere in this book. Certainly, however, the cruise provided us with a wonderful opportunity for extending and enriching those skills which are the linking factor in all our study schemes.

REPORT ON COOPERATION BETWEEN DEPARTMENTS IN A GIRLS' SECONDARY SCHOOL IN SCOTLAND

Although only a small group with two staff actually went on the cruise others were involved and the Modern Studies Department developed a project round the cruise for classes remaining behind.

The main part of the school instruction was centred on the compilation of a scrapbook on the actual cruise. The school group taking part in the cruise was divided into four separate sections each one responsible for getting information and material about one particular place, for their section of the scrapbook. The staff of the Modern Studies Department gave lessons in school on different aspects of the countries to be visited and the pupils did individual research into 'interesting facts, costumes and customs' including the collection of material for the scrapbook from newspapers, magazines, radio and TV programmes. Some girls chose needlework as a 'voluntary activity' for the cruise under the guidance of the Homecraft Staff who also helped with preliminary thought to costumes and ideas for carnival night on board.

The Commerce Department supervised the cutting and duplicating of stencils by pupils in connection with the venture; the reproduction of short notes on places to be visited and the provision of folders for each pupil.

The Maths Department assisted with the production of exchange rates ready reckoners and the preparation of individual money cards for the withdrawal of pocket money from the Party Leader while on board.

The Music Department chose the songs and rehearsed the girls as a choir for the Cruise Concert.

STUDY OF AJACCIO BY A PARTY FROM A BOYS' GRAMMAR SCHOOL

(Although much of the work for the next project was done aboard or ashore, the preliminary study could equally well have been undertaken in school and the projects illustrate how different aspects of what might be described as a social or environmental study are brought together. As there are certain administrative problems implicit in this approach it would be advisable to check the position first with the B.I. Senior Education Officer because it might involve departing from the ship's rules for shore parties).

Before the cruise, the group leader wrote to the Mayor of Ajaccio explaining the study which the students wanted to undertake ashore. This study, to be carried out in groups, was to cover subjects suggested by the boys themselves:

The comparative cost of living
Industry and trade
Local government
Education
Communications
Entertainment and sport

The Mayor replied very fully giving the addresses of people who would be prepared to help either in correspondence or with an interview during the visit. Each group then wrote, in French, to several people in Ajaccio and most letters were answered. This was followed by group discussions on how to develop each enquiry. The amount of time devoted to preliminary study, discussion and background reading would depend on the time available within the school programme.

The headings of the ground covered and information collected during the visit illustrate possible lines for the expansion of information and further research verbally or by means of layouts of visual material.

The work in Ajaccio
This is given below under the subject headings:

Group A   Subject: Cost of living

1 Visited Manager of the Banque de France. Taped part of the conversation.
2 Toured shops and markets collecting prices of goods.

Group B   Subject: Industry and trade

1 Conversation with policeman in order to find fish market. Noted names of the different fish.
2 Asked about types of food in food market. Enquired into location and types of vineyard in Corsica. Obtained wine labels from a store with information on wine-making.
3 Talked to owners of an iron foundry; to a coffee grinder and to some assistants in shops.
4 Enquired about tourist trade at Syndicat d'Initiative. Collected leaflets.
5 Went to two travel agents and a car hire firm.
6 Interviewed Secretary General of Chamber of Commerce and Industry.

Group C   Subject: Local government

1 Went to prefecture to keep appointment with M. Lebeschu, the Joint Prefect. The policeman on guard refused the group admission because they were a day late.
2 Visited Hôtel de Ville, asked questions and were given leaflets.

Group D   Subject: Education

1 Visited Education College of Les Salins. Toured mechanised workshop, craft shop, metalwork shop and electronics room. The group was taken on by car to the next school.
2 Visited Laetitia Bonaparte School. Interviewed Headmistress. Shown round by English teacher. Made notes on medical room, dining rooms, kitchen, dormitories, laboratories. Noted the numbers of staff and of pupils and took photographs.

Group E   Subject: Communications

1 Roads (*a*) Took 5-minute traffic census of cars entering and leaving the town, noting makes.
      (*b*) Visited garage.
2 Rail   Visited station. Obtained a timetable but no posters.
3 Air   Visited Air France Bureau as the airfield was too far away. Obtained timetable.
4 Sea   Obtained maps giving some information on this. Obtained pamphlets from Syndicat d'Initiative. Visited harbour and saw cable-layer dock. Estimated that harbour would be for ships of 10,000 tons or more.

Group F.   Subject: Entertainment and sport

1 Entertainment   Visited 'Empire Cinema', interviewed the manager and shown around. Noted seat prices and were told average number of customers per year. Discussed types of film. Obtained posters.
2 Sport   Interviewed director of sport department. Noted the sports

played and watched and the numbers of clubs of different sorts available. Encountered language difficulties and this took a very long time.

Note: This group was second year.

AN INDIVIDUAL APPROACH FROM A SCHOOL

'The Holy Land Cruise had a tremendous, revitalising effect on the work of the whole Department.'

In addition to block or charter bookings many schools book on their own each year. Unfortunately it is impossible to give a full account of the variety of experiences of schools who book independently. The following describes the tradition of educational cruising in one London grammar school from which the Party Leader, head of the Religious Education Department, has taken students for the past seven years. She selects the cruise best suited to her syllabus and follows the B.I. Programme both on board and for shore visits but her plans may include extra shore excursions during the period for optional visits, by special arrangement with B.I. If the party are 'O' and 'A' level candidates she chooses a cruise during the school holidays. Recently she has taken second and third year students during term time.

When a party books individually it is an advantage, some would say essential, for the Party Leader to have had previous experience of an educational cruise and to be assisted by a colleague who also knows the students. It may be stating the obvious but when branching out on special shore excursions, not part of the B.I. programme, the Party Leader needs to know the area and its potentialities and to have visited all the 'objectives' on a previous occasion. If numbers justify a private coach it is advisable to ask for this to be laid on, preferably with an English-speaking driver, when making final reservations for the cruise. When public transport is used it is an advantage to have someone in the party who speaks the language and to have had recent experience of how the public transport system operates. Unauthorised local guides are to be avoided. Students need to be well briefed beforehand on what they may expect to find in the locality, and to make the most of the short time ashore they may get greater satisfaction from studying a few things in depth.

If the cruise is chosen to help 'O' and 'A' level candidates who will be sitting papers in Religious Knowledge or the history of the Renaissance or the geography of the Mediterranean basin, they will be 'familiar with the text' but the classroom periods on board enable students to rehearse what they are going to see and, afterwards, to discuss and record their findings.

It is interesting to recount how this particular enterprise developed. Impressed by the influence on her pupils of her own visit to the Holy Land, the Party Leader decided in 1965 to take a group to Israel. She contacted every travel agent in London but the cost was out of reach.

By a coincidence she noticed a B.I. brochure in the Staff Room which included a trip to the Holy Land. A telephone call to the B.I. Senior Education Officer began a practice from which several hundred girls in her school have since benefited.

In collaboration with other departments, the choice of cruises to the Holy Land, Italy and Greece has been linked with syllabuses in Art, Architecture, Classics, History, Geography and Religious Knowledge. It may be unusual to select a cruise most likely to bring reality to the examination syllabus and, administratively, this approach could not be adopted for all parties. But the advantages are considerable, not only in the examination results but in the enthusiasm shared by those not able to go who take part in the preparatory visits to the British Museum, Greenwich, Hampton Court or National Art Galleries and join the discussion when the party returns; in the cooperation achieved between different subject departments and in the influence of these visits on choice of careers. For some, the educational cruise to the Holy Land has helped to reaffirm their faith; for others, now teaching Religious Education, it offers the hope of taking parties themselves.

The party, whether it goes to Leghorn with an extra over-night stop in Florence to study Renaissance art at 'A' level or to Ephesus for those studying the Acts of the Apostles at 'O' level, will not be exclusively concerned with 'examination requirements' because every cruise offers broader studies and if there are any spare places they will be available to girls in the same age group on the understanding that serious work is expected of them.

As an illustration, one group of fifth-formers made a tape/slide programme on their return to school during the period after 'O' level and before the end of term. This programme was based on material collected during the visit to the Holy Land at Easter. The Easter story was illustrated by readings from the New Testament illustrated with slides and descriptions of the actual places seen during the visit in the correct sequence of the story. This group of girls affirmed, however, that it was not until they began studying for 'A' level that the real significance of their experiences was evident.

AN INDIVIDUAL APPROACH FROM A LOCAL EDUCATION AUTHORITY

In planning their second cruise a Local Education Authority in the Midlands decided to base this on two themes; first the volcanic activity in the Mediterranean region, and the latest theories of geomorphology and geophysics and, second, the historical consequences of the volcanic activity in the area. They were assisted by a university lecturer and former H.M. Inspector well versed in Minoan and Mycenaean culture. The passage included Naples for Vesuvius and Pompeii, Syracuse via Stromboli and the Lipari Islands from which the students visited Etna; Crete, Santorin – the volcano presumed to be responsible for the decline of the Minoan culture, from there to Athens and Nauplia to see Mycenae and then home from Venice. This involved a very tight, possibly exhausting, fortnight with much of the travelling done at night as a deliberate experiment.

The third cruise organised by this L.E.A. with 850 students from their own county, average age fifteen to sixteen, and 100 from two other Authorities, was intended to follow up the theme of vol-canicity and plate tectonics. The ship left and returned to South-ampton cruising through the Western Isles and Hebrides and calling at Reykjavik, Surtsey, Olden and Oslo. By visiting both Iceland and Norway they were able to reinforce the parallel historic theme – The Vikings. A member of the Executive Committee of the Scottish National Trust and University and College of Education lecturers, specialists in the fields of animal life in the Hebrides, geophysics, glaciology, ecology, marine biology and history, joined the edu-cational staff.

Since the most interesting things to be seen in Iceland are not within range of a day trip it was decided that those students who wished, 500 altogether, should spend one night ashore and split up into four separate expeditions. The first expedition to Landmanna-laugar, an active volcanic area, had a geological basis. The second, with a bias towards glaciology, went along the south coast to study at close quarters the glacier that comes down from the Mydrals Jokull. The third party went to Hveravellir in the centre of the island. Although this is also an active volcanic area their main theme was ecology. The fourth party, interested in history, made a tour of the area of Iceland mentioned in the sagas. This adventure theme was continued in Norway when all the students and all the Party Leaders left the ship and camped for one night at the foot of the Briksdal Glacier, near Olden.

The cruise ran a voluntary course on marine biology during the time at sea. Samples were taken with dredging equipment at Reykjavik, Olden and Oslo. Sea-bed cores were obtained from an area off Ulla-pool and another just north of the Faroes, which could be related to the volcanic studies; recent eruptions and the ash layers in the mud.

SUBJECT STUDIES

There is no limit to the way in which experiences from the cruise and observation of a ship at sea can be related to the curriculum. The next section expands some ideas received from individual teachers and guest lecturers, under subject headings. They are in no way authorita-tive or comprehensive, and in some ways show a personal bias. At the least they may help to provoke discussion.

Art and architecture

It would be rash to suggest in detail ways in which an educational cruise might open new vistas in art education; they are too numerous to mention in a short book. Whether the interest be in the appreciation of architecture, painting or sculpture or in natural forms, objects or people, visual sensitivity is helped by earlier study.

Many of the cities within the itinerary will offer scope for a study of art history in considerable depth – from pre-Christian times to the mid-twentieth century according to the particular glories of Athens, Ephesus, Amsterdam, Florence, and Venice or Oslo where the more contemporary Vigeland Park offers a lively theme for group discussion. In places which lack 'Old Masters' there are many local art forms in buildings, boats, carts, and leatherware, pottery and the way in which food and other goods are displayed in shops or on the market stall.

Visits to local museums, art galleries and historic houses, many of which reflect trends in European art offer pre-cruise preparation. Some schools arrange a 'trial run'; a visit, preferably on foot, to look at the local cathedral or even industrial scene and in looking learn how to use one's eyes. Much of this work can be supported by books at the right levels, for example, for sixth forms, Kenneth Clark's *Civilization*, and carefully selected prints, films and television programmes. But, at the end of the day, this is a very personal business dependent not so much on the places to be visited as on the enthusiasm of the teacher.

Astronomy
Space flight has aroused much more interest in astronomy than ever before. The best viewing point when at sea is the foredeck, since it is kept in total darkness to make navigation easier. Of the constellations many students will be able to recognise Ursa Major (the Plough). This is a good starting point. As the ship sails southwards from these shores constellations which do not normally rise high enough above the horizon in England begin to appear. At sea there will be little or no air pollution such as industrial haze so that stars can often be seen within a degree of the horizon. In this overpopulated island a large number of students live within the range of streetlight glare so that to be able to seek out entirely new constellations will be a fascinating experience. Like all other aspects of educational cruising, pre-cruise preparation will pay dividends.[1] This is particularly true in the case of astronomy, one of the 'out-of-school' activities encouraged on board and supervised by a ship's officer.

This growing interest in astronomy, first expressed in a request from a Party Leader, 'Please suggest what I can do with my girls on deck at night', has been encouraged through an arrangement with the Director of the London Planetarium to visit the Planetarium for a special lecture on the night sky as it will be seen in the relevant latitudes during the cruise. This is followed up by a demonstration, on board, by certain officers previously schooled in astronomy. The

1 See *Nautical Studies for Educational Cruising* by Joyce and Lionel O. Joseph, 1968 Sea and Airborne Education, Lorengau Cottage, Forest Green, Dorking, Surrey (supplied direct).

Director of the London Planetarium also provides slides and charts of the heavens. So successful has this project been and so enthusiastic the response of all concerned that astronomy is a regular feature of many cruises, and one of the officers involved has been elected a Fellow of the Royal Astronomical Society.

It might be prudent to point out, however, that there is little point in dealing at any length with astronomy or arranging a planetarium visit for pupils proceeding on a northern cruise, since the extended daylight of Scandinavia in the summer months, when such cruises take place, makes observation impossible.

Classical studies

References throughout the book make it unnecessary to include a separate note on the way in which the Ancient World becomes a reality through educational cruises, a point emphasised by Sir John Wolfenden in Chapter 7. This gives support to the growing interest in schools in non-linguistic courses in classical studies like the Cambridge School Classics Project to introduce classical civilisation to pupils of all abilities in the eleven to thirteen age-group and to the movement towards establishing syllabuses in classical studies higher up the school in their own right or as part of an 'integrated' humanities scheme. The Cambridge School Classics Project was initiated by the Nuffield Foundation in 1966 and subsequently funded by the Schools Council. The bibliography on page 111 lists a few of the many books, both fiction and non-fiction, and other materials for pre-cruise study.

English

(The English language is rich in poetry and prose connected with the sea. Choice of reading is a personal business often reflecting the trends of the time. As an example of the richness of the literature on which some teachers and students may wish to draw, Dr Ronald Hope, editor of *The Harrap Book of Sea Verse* and, over the years, a frequent guest lecturer on the *Nevasa* and *Uganda*, has contributed the following section.)

For the teacher of English language and literature B.I. school cruising offers so many opportunities that it is difficult to know where to begin. 'Nobly, nobly Cape Saint Vincent to the north-west died away' takes on a new significance when on board the sunset can actually be seen running, 'reeking into Cadiz Bay'. And Chaucer's shipman lives more vividly when 'all the havens, as they were, from Gotland to the Cape of Finistere' are familiar to the reader.

Add to the *Harrap Book of Sea Verse* Captain Eric Bush's anthology *Flowers of the Sea,* a useful source book for prose passages about ships and seafarers and Stan Hugill's *Shanties from the Seven Seas* and any teacher of English has material enough to devise a programme for the classroom, and for school or shipboard entertainment.

Moreover, these books offer a variety which will ensure participation from all pupils, particularly if a guitarist or a few recorder players are available.

From the wealth of English maritime writing, both prose and poetry, every teacher will be able to cull his own bouquet, and the choice will be determined in part by the pupils with whom he is concerned. Some years ago Oliver Warner wrote a pamphlet on *English Maritime Writing* for the British Council, and more recently the School Library Association has published *Books and the Sea,* an annotated list of modern books on the sea and shipping. The Department of Education and Science has also produced, in Education Pamphlet No. 44, a booklet called *The Sea in Education,* though this is not written specifically for English teachers. All these may be of help in providing the teacher with ideas, though ideas concerning the sea in English literature are not hard to come by. After all, one professor wrote a book recently to suggest that Shakespeare himself was a sailor, and was so knowledgeable about the sea because during those missing years in his personal history he was away fighting the Armada!

Whether Shakespeare was a sailor or not, *The Tempest* was certainly inspired in part by the early accounts of Raleigh's attempt to colonise North America, and the writings of the Elizabethans, many of them gathered together by Hakluyt, are graphic enough to interest most young people if carefully selected. Drake's *The World Encompassed* (from 'the Notes of Master Francis Fletcher, Preacher'), for example, is short, simply written and enthralling.

Perhaps this is not the place to dwell on sea literature in general, but almost any seaman's memoirs are worth reading, from *The Observations of Sir Richard Hawkins,* through Edward Barlow's *Journal,* Cook's *Voyages,* and Dana's *Two Years before the Mast* to David Bone's *The Brassbounder* and the late Sir James Bisset's trilogy, including *Sail Ho!,* which he wrote after his retirement as Commodore of Cunard. Seafarers usually use a good plain English style, all shipshape and Bristol fashion, which can be read with pleasure at any age.

Is Captain Marryat's *Peter Simple* still widely read? It remains one of the funniest novels in the English language. Smollett's *Roderick Random* is a stimulating introduction to the eighteenth-century picaresque novel. *Moby Dick* and Conrad – like Walt Whitman among the poets – want very careful handling, though *Typhoon* and *The Nigger of the Narcissus* can prove splendid in the classroom, and among the playwright's work Eugene O'Neill's one-act plays (not to mention *The Iceman Cometh*) should not be overlooked. In the commercial theatre O'Neill is too much neglected, although the National Theatre Company has staged *A Long Day's Journey into Night.*

With particular cruises in view the teacher of English will not want to confine himself to the literature of the sea. With a Scandinavian cruise in prospect, and thinking of O'Neill, who was so much influenced by them, an exploration of the dramatic works of Ibsen and

Strindberg would not be out of place. If the ship is going to call at Leningrad, not only does the whole of Russian literature take on a new relevance, but point is given to the works of all those English and other European travellers who have been to Russia in the past. On the way home, on the Danish coast, Elsinore may well come into view, and one is back with *Hamlet*, or even *Rosencrantz and Guildenstern are Dead*. If planning or pre-planning extends to films, Shakespeare and Strindberg can be brought together by hiring Sir Laurence Olivier's films of *Hamlet* and *The Dance of Death,* while if Russia has been on the itinerary the Russian *Hamlet* can be added for good measure.

At the other end of the cruising world – in the eastern Mediterranean – the horizons extend even further. 'When I last saw Waring . . .' Browning begins, and goes on: 'We were sailing by Trieste'. Many other English poets have sailed by Trieste, Genoa, Venice, and on to the isles of Greece and the Greek mainland. Shelley, Keats, Byron . . ., both poetry and prose, offer many opportunities. From Renaissance times down to James Elroy Flecker and Lawrence Durrell a host of privileged English writers and travellers have gone east to all those exotic places where, for the fairly modest price of a school journey, thousands of children aboard *Uganda* and *Nevasa* now have the opportunity to follow in their wake.

And two or three thousand years before the Renaissance and the English travellers there were the seafarers who inspired the beginnings of European literature. European literature begins with Homer, and Homer begins with the Greek heroes who sailed to Troy, into the Black Sea and, above all, into the western Mediterranean. Is it possible that they even sailed to England? At least a few brave spirits in Homer's own day seem to have gone beyond the Pillars of Hercules and sailed upon the 'River of Ocean' to strange and foggy climes. They had heard too of places where days and nights could last for months.

Through *The Odyssey*, in any of the marvellous translations that we have, the teacher of English can bring the whole story of European civilisation together. As friend, philosopher and guide do not overlook Ernle Bradford's *Ulysses Found*, an excellent detective story in its own right, for Bradford, like Ulysses, covers much of the ground of almost any eastern Mediterranean cruise.

> Oft of one wide expanse had I been told
> That deep-browed Homer ruled as his demesne.

We, too, can look into Chapman (or Rieu) with a wild surmise, for it is seafaring that brings Homer and Keats and stout Cortez – and the Icelandic sagas, the Celtic sagas, and the Greek myths – all together. A school cruise has as much to offer to the teacher of English as it has to the teacher of history and geography.

Some examples of the stimulus given by a cruise to young people's observations and thus to their original writing are given in Chapter 8. To a large extent this comes after the preparation and build-up and during and after the cruise itself. The world and the classroom are never the same again!

Geography
The preparatory work will vary from school to school but, to suggest the obvious, the more background a student has of the countries to be visited the better; the more it will assist the practical work which can be done ashore and afloat. It is probably in the realm of some of the more specialised and developing branches of geography that educational cruises, be they in the Arctic, the Baltic, or the Mediterranean, offer most. Geology can become a reality not just a series of heavy dots, oblique lines and hatchings on a complicated map from which it is almost impossible to relate the shape and colour of rock formations in practice. Information briefs prepared for a Local Education Authority cruise in 1971 show the structure on which preparatory work might be based:

Vulcanology
Weather in the Azores, Canary and Madeira Islands: the different weather patterns found in the British Isles and the Atlantic Islands visited by the Cruise.

The sea fishing industries of the Iberian Peninsula: trawling, seine netting, long lining, jigging and other methods which can be identified in port if not at sea.

Geological setting of the islands of the Eastern North Atlantic leading to suggestions for further reading, the making of simple clinometers and the collection of rock samples to show variety of volcanic products.

The position of the Atlantic Islands: their climate, strategic and geological significance. This preparatory brief sets the scene for studies to be carried out during the cruise:

1 Redraw diagram of angle of noonday sun's rays for Madeira and Azores. Verify this angle during cruise by measuring shadow of an upright stick at local noon and applying trigonometry to a right-angled triangle.

2 Calculate longitude during cruise by finding local noon and comparing with a watch set to G.M.T. (Note: Portugal keeps G.M.T. as its standard time.) Local noon can be found by plotting the length of a shadow from an upright stick. Local noon is when the shadow of the stick is at its minimum length. This could give purpose to sunbathing for half an hour either side of local noon.

3 Observe wind direction and speed at a known position during each day of the cruise. One way of entering the results is by drawing a circular graph with bearing on the circular scale and latitude on the radial scale. Plot each day's observation with a numbered dot. Wind strength and direction might be shown by a form of wind rose.

4 On an outline of the North Atlantic mark the oceanic circulation and some well known voyages, e.g. Columbus, Triangular Trade Route of seventeenth and eighteenth centuries, relevant parts of Sir Francis

Chichester's single-handed voyage around the world, Thor Heyerdahl's voyage in *Ra II*.

5 Complete the names of the individual islands on the accompanying maps of the island groups.

Many schools prepare geography work sheets on which students can record observations while they are on shore and then compile more detailed notes when they return to the ship. The Observation and Recollection Sheets issued by B.I. are a useful basis for this method of enquiry, ranging from 'The Port: What activities did you observe (*a*) in the ship and (*b*) on shore, as the ship approached the quay', to 'the Town: What was the density of the traffic; did it drive on the right or left; were the vehicles British or foreign makes; was the traffic well controlled; was the control by police or lights or both; how were the police dressed; were there any pedestrian crossings?' and 'What articles did you buy and how much did you pay for them?'

History

Some schools continue to emphasise English political history but today a broader approach is usually followed, which may include local and social history, European and world studies. These trends are reflected in the growing popularity of museums, particularly those with collections expressing social life and customs and in the efforts to enrich history teaching through the use of radio and television, history 'kits', document wallets, historical films, replicas and historical novels.

One of the first lectures on board is an historical background to the cruises. The Mediterranean, Baltic or Atlantic seaport countries are put into a general European perspective.

These lectures help to highlight common themes and historical events in the countries to be visited. Apart from background lectures, each port lecture contains historical references and to these it is possible to add more material in independent sightseeing time ashore, as well as on the guided tours.

The introduction to this book describes how educational cruises can bring history alive. Visits to the shores of Italy, Greece and Tunisia in the space of fourteen days will give a fresh meaning to bald phrases in history books such as, 'In Roman times North Africa was the granary of Europe'. Of the parts of the world covered by B.I. Cruises, the Mediterranean provides so many opportunities for studying the foundations of western civilisation it is possible to mention only a few headings from the programme of one county expedition: famous Greeks, myths and legends; the Greek alphabet, Greek drama and costume; the rise of the Roman Empire, Italian history, the Early Church, Byzantine art and architecture, the Greek Orthodox Church, Islam and navigation in the ancient world.

At first sight, Spain, Portugal and the Azores might not appear to offer quite such a wealth of studies but the information briefs from another Local Education Authority Cruise show how far this is from the truth. It requires little imagination to understand the possibilities for following the influence of Portuguese discoveries on English history and on the future development of the world. This can be more dramatically brought home if the students see for themselves.

When the *Nevasa* sails up the Tagus in the early morning of the 12 July next year you will see from the port side one of the most splendid monuments in the world. It is the prow of a ship surrounded by figures of Prince Henry the Navigator and the sea captains and explorers who lived in the great age of Portugal. It epitomises not only strenuous endeavour but one of the supreme periods of change in the history of the world, which may be compared with the present age in which space exploration is creating a new dimension for men's activities.

A cruise is an admirable starting point for studying maritime history. 'It is not our conquests', wrote Lewis Roberts in the seventeenth century, 'but our commerce; it is not our swords, but our sayls, that first spred the English name in Barbary, and thence came into Turkey, Armenia, Moscovia, Arabia, Persia, India, China, and indeed over and about the world.' And in our own day, Arnold Toynbee has written that the fifteenth-century, western European invention of a ship that could stay at sea for months on end changed western Europe from what he calls a cul-de-sac of civilisation to a roundabout: trade that had flowed overland on camelback to the Mediterranean now began to flow seaward in the hold of a ship to Spain, Portugal, France, the Low Countries and to Britain.

Well before the fifteenth century, and fitting almost any cruise itinerary, are the fascinating problems of how and when the Mediterranean basin was opened up, who first sailed into the Atlantic and how far, whether there was an independent development of maritime enterprise in British waters as far back as Megalithic times, who first explored northwards and westwards from Britain, what did the Vikings contribute, and so on. A new dimension is added to most historical periods if they are looked at through a sailor's eyes.

But sometimes the emphasis will be less on historical concepts, and endeavour on the grand scale, than on more intimate projects such as the work submitted by a pupil in a Surrey school for the Certificate of Secondary Education in which she made a study of a century of childhood life in her own village, partly through interviews with successive generations, and extended this to interviewing people at ports of call. She used a portable tape recorder, often more suitable than the written word for this kind of project.

Mathematics and navigation

Some itineraries offer a historical approach to mathematics in the study of the lives and influence of great mathematicians, particularly where the cruise is visiting the birth place or a city associated with their work, like Syracuse.

All cruises present practical opportunities for 'high finance' in foreign currency calculations and many for bartering in the Souk. According to gossip students base their deductions about the cost of living in different countries on the fluctuations in price of a bottle of Coca-Cola.

On bartering, perhaps it might be worthwhile to strike a note of warning. A student from an industrial city in the North found himself in a tricky situation in the main market in Athens: 'I saw a pair of slippers outside a stall in the Plaka with the figure 36 on them,' he said. 'I thought that meant 36 drachmas (50p), so I offered the man 30. 'But 36 was the size, and they really cost over 100 drachmas. The shopkeeper was so cross he picked up the slippers and banged me on the head with them, then pushed me out of the store.'

A good deal of mathematical work is based on ships and shipping including tonnage (displacement tonnage, dead weight tonnage, gross register tonnage, net register tonnage), speed and earning capacity. Good navigation depends on four factors:

1 Geometrical understanding, particularly of relationships between lengths and angles in spherical trigonometry as applied to the earth.
2 Accurate charts, maps and astronomical information.
3 Scientific aids, including the traditional navigational instruments of compasses, ship's log, chronometer and sextant, as well as modern devices such as radar and the Decca Navigator, and
4 Correct observation, calculation and interpretation of information which will make the visit to the bridge more memorable.

A Party Leader with long experience of educational cruises describes navigation on board and the interesting work which can be done with groups ranging from ten-year-olds on board for the first time to eighteen-year-olds already destined for a career at sea.

The taking of compass bearings with an ex-W.D. marching compass is simple enough, plotting them on the chart is even simpler; net result to the ten-year-old student, 'I am here', and he or she will derive much satisfaction from doing just that. When the same exercise has been completed by the rest of the party and all results (fixes) have been linked one to another, there is the ship's course. The time taken from the first position to the last will enable the speed of the ship to be calculated. If this differs radically from the service speed of the ship, then either the Captain has reduced speed to keep to his estimated time of arrival or, more likely, a current is holding the ship back, or conversely carrying her forward or sideways. Students will therefore want to know something about tides and currents.

Tides are, in general, a surface flow of water caused by the pull of celestial bodies, the moon and the sun. Currents are the mass movement of water in the oceans caused by convection and the earth's rotation and to a lesser extent, in some areas, by prevailing winds. Land masses will often cause divergence as in the case of the Gulf Stream which later becomes the North Atlantic Drift. In shallow waters it is probably tidal flow which causes variations from service speed, while in deep waters currents are usually responsible. Published tidal information and current flows will normally provide the answer (see Admiralty tide tables).

Other methods of fixing position are also within the scope of the younger students. Transits, produced by two conspicuous objects ashore appearing in line with each other, can be drawn as position lines on the chart and will indicate that the ship is somewhere along that line. Such exercises can be extended through the visit to the bridge, where not only will the students see what has been done for the purpose of their safety, but they can also ask for ranges and bearings from the Plan Position Indicator (P.P.I.) of the radar set.

The many instruments seen on the bridge and in the engine room give untold scope for the explanation of the practical use of principles and concepts taught in the physics laboratory. For the junior pupil this can be as simple as the echo of sound used to find the depth of water beneath the ship, whilst at the other end of the age range the calculations and principles involved in the hyperbolic fixing systems, such as the Decca Navigator, will extend the best student.

Although students will see the register to the ship's log on the bridge giving a record of the distance run through the water and possibly the speed in knots, the old Dutchman's Log principle can be adopted for practical work by the party. One hundred and one feet marked out on the deck, using two fixed objects aboard as sights, will make the calculation of speed, from the time taken for flotsam to pass from one end of the measured distance to the other, very simple. The time in seconds for the flotsam to pass, divided into 60 = knots, i.e. 4 seconds = 15 knots. It is unlikely that the nautical mile will be 'metricated' as this distance is based on one minute of latitude and for that there is no metric equivalent which would make calculation easier.

Simple sextants are available on board and can be used for many exercises. Position finding in coastal waters by the horizontal sextant angle method, using tracing paper as a temporary station pointer, can be as simple or advanced as the ability of the party permits. Older students can tackle a noon sight which will give a position in terms of latitude and longitude. To achieve this, when all that can be seen is the sun and the heaving of the waves to the horizon, gives a real sense of achievement to any boy or girl.

Modern languages

Seen in the overall perspective of educational visits abroad, educational cruises offer less opportunity for speaking foreign languages, unless it is a mixed cruise with other nationalities, than exchange visits or one of the many language courses organised for young people in other European countries. But some language preparation is helpful. B.I. produce language sheets for the countries visited and schools are encouraged, with the help of the language teacher, to make tapes for special practice of phrases including greetings, asking the way, shopping, money, key facts about yourself.

There will be many opportunities for collecting 'realia' which, when brought back to school, can be 'exploited' in the language lesson especially if the visit is to countries whose language is taught in school, and used as valuable material for background studies. Newspapers, admission tickets to museums and art galleries, sugar wrappers and sweet papers will have their use in school or classroom collections; but like other material for 'resource collections' they need to be carefully identified and documented.

When itineraries include France, La Pallice and La Rochelle, for example, arrangements may be made for French students of English from the Lycees and Colleges to act as guides to the visiting groups. The Modern Language Adviser of one Authority has commented: 'These duties they undertook with pleasure and distinction, and these young people were in turn welcomed on board the ship as guests of the Company. This provided a welcome opportunity for our children to mix with young French people, an opportunity which they thoroughly enjoyed.'

Physical education on board

It is often the practice for a County Physical Education Adviser to accompany the Local Education Authority cruise as a member of the L.E.A. staff. He or she will be responsible for preparing a timetable each day so that the deck games periods are fully used and every student has a variety of activity during the cruise. The P.E. Adviser will also choose the Party Leaders to take charge of deck games. To assist, some L.E.A.s select two teachers in training from Colleges of Education where they run main courses for physical education.

If the L.E.A. does not wish to make its own arrangements B.I. provide assistance. Through a regular scheme with Dartford College of Physical Education and, for Scottish cruises, Dunfermline College, two students are attached on a rota system, to each of the school ships as part of their teaching practice.

One-sixth of all students, about 150 youngsters, will be engaged in deck games at any time during the working day and the wonder is how many vigorous activities are provided within the inevitably limited deck space. On the *Nevasa*, for example, there are two pitches for deck hockey and five pitches for deck quoits on the Promenade Deck aft and space for either volley ball, deck hockey or deck tennis, aft.

On A Deck, forward, there is a swimming pool for twenty students and two courts for deck tennis and deck quoits. On A Deck aft there are six tables for table tennis.

There is also a limited area for skipping, medicine ball, keep fit and deck quoits. But add to the natural limitations of space for such activities on board any ship, the fact that the swimming pool is likely to be out of action in bad weather or in coastal waters and that, on the *Nevasa*, the Promenade Deck aft is over the Assembly Hall and is not available for deck hockey because of the noise when the Assembly Hall is in use, it will be appreciated that the control and organisation of games is a highly complex and skilled operation. For this reason there have to be some pretty tough rules for ship's games which, besides those mentioned, may also include tug-of-war, 'continuous cricket', water polo and 'crab football'.

With the current emphasis on outdoor activities which are a challenge to the individual rather than fiercely competitive, some students not imbued with a desire to play competitive games may find the tug-of-war or deck hockey less attractive than happily occupying the swimming pool. In a survey published in the ship's magazine on one cruise, students were asked, 'Which pastime do you prefer: swimming, deck hockey and cricket, or deck quoits and tennis?' Fifty per cent of the boys and none of the girls chose deck hockey and cricket and thirty per cent of both boys and girls chose deck quoits and tennis. But if in the pre-cruise preparation the students are aware of the problems of organising physical activities within a confined space, these restrictions may be readily seen as demanding unselfishness and self-discipline – old fashioned but durable virtues.

Resource collections

In the last few years, sets of books, museum exhibits, even 'the nature table' have emerged as Resource Collections. Resource Centres have been set up and become the object of research projects. They mean different things in different contexts but usually include duplicated sheets, maps, charts, illustrations, press cuttings, slides, tapes together with models, museum items, books and journals. Much of the material is produced by the teachers themselves or by the children. A Resource Centre, whether it is within the school or serves a number of schools, implies the systematic production, storage and use of the collection.

In some schools, before the cruise party sets off, it is possible to give a special briefing on the contribution students can make to the school collection.

Photographs form a useful part of any collection especially if there is careful planning, including the formation of teams of photographers whose job it is to cover different aspects of the places to be seen; roads, buildings, unusual transport, imports and exports, unfamiliar crops, flora and fauna.

Methods of recording information on tape, black-and-white prints, colour slides and film are discussed and arrangements made to supply some film and tape from school funds. Where this has been done the school has found that the more thought is put into the building up of resource collections, both as an exercise in audio-visual education and the classification and organisation of material, the better. This may call for cooperation from both the school librarian and the audio-visual aids specialist but the results will have a value, not only to the immediate participants, but to future members of the school. Experience has shown that it is important to try and be precise about the location of shots; to avoid the inevitable post-cruise doubts, 'Was *that* on top of the Acropolis or in the amphitheatre at Ephesus?' and to anticipate in detail the item's future interest and use, irrespective of the original purpose for which it was collected.

One Party Leader has offered a helpful comment:

Customs regulations may prevent the large scale importation of roots and soil specimens and the temptation to 'lift' archaeological finds is to be avoided but there is scope for the collection of fossils, lava and other geological specimens and some schools may think it is worthwhile to put aside funds for the collection of carefully selected local crafts.

Science and marine biology

An educational cruise is sometimes the means of extending pupils' investigations in science. While a study of flora and fauna, marine biology and experiments on pressure, temperature and salinity of the sea are obvious choices, particularly interesting for students who are normally land-bound, others could link up with themes suggested in *Nuffield Secondary Science*[1] and similar Projects; for example, Interdependence of Living Things, Movement and the Earth, and Earth's Place in the Universe. The periods ashore are often too short to allow much chance of doing any serious ecological studies although simple comparisons of habitat might be possible. Ideas for developing this are discussed in the final chapter, 'The Way Ahead'.

Two experienced Party Leaders have written about the work they have done from the ship:

There is always a chance that a 'blow' will occur sometime during a cruise. The radio announcement 'The Meteorological Office issues the following gale warning to shipping at . . .' takes on a new meaning both before and more especially after a cruise. The natural elements, weather and sea, affect each other. For example the disparity in temperature between that of a sea water sample, taken from over the side when standing on the fo'c'sle (pollution farther aft) and that of the air at the same time, may well reveal the reason for the occurrence of fog at sea in what may appear to be fine weather conditions. Such samples may also be used for checking salinity and pH value. In the former a higher reading than the accepted norm of thirty-five parts per thousand in certain areas may suggest a high rate of evaporation, whilst a lower figure will be due in all probability to a high inflow of fresh water. Typical examples of this are the Mediterranean and Baltic seas respectively.

Such discrepancies also reflect on the flora and fauna of the sea in the particular area concerned. Plankton in samples will vary from one area to another. Students aboard the first school ship *Dunera* found over forty copepods, which are about the size of the print on this page, in a pint of sea water taken off North Cape, whereas in southern Biscay, it was often difficult to find any at all. It is not necessary of course to wait until aboard to obtain samples of plankton. A little exploration of the gut during the dissection of a herring will reveal some very interesting fauna. This simple dissection

1 *Nuffield Secondary Science*, Organiser: Hilda Misselbrook, published by Longman, for the Nuffield Foundation 1971.

can help students understand more about conditions and life in the sea than any amount of chalk and talk. The use of buoyancy devices in pelagic fish leads naturally into a study of bathe-contours and, while many students are familiar with ordinary height contours, they are not so well acquainted with those below sea level. The making of relief models brings a touch of reality to the sea bed 'topography'; for instance an orthodox scale model of the Bay of Biscay shows very clearly the 2700 fathoms down to 'Davey Jones's locker'. Similarly cross-sections of Norwegian Fjords, based on chart soundings, can be very instructive, particularly in respect of the deeper water within the fjord compared with that at the threshold.

Much marine study is closely allied to geography and to geology. Geology makes coastlines, and the sea bed is geology in the making as well as geology of the past. Much information relating to this subject is readily found alongside the soundings marked on the Admiralty chart. In ports of call so much of what is seen in architecture and the surrounding countryside can be directly related to the underlying strata and the formation of the earth's crust.

A marine biologist has written an account of her cruise memories which illustrates the way in which the educational cruise can give students direct practical knowledge and experience

Owing to great foresight and planning, a large number of preserved marine specimens were available for the thirty boys and girls to look at, sort through and so gain some idea of life in the sea, before they ventured into the dark unknown on their first 'live' trip, in one of the ship's lifeboats, into Malaga harbour.

We went at night: it is a biological fact that microscopic organisms tend to rise to the surface at night, but as a practical venture, after that experience, I am not so sure. One does not often find oneself in pitch blackness – but we did at sea that night as we chugged farther and farther away from the friendly gay lights of the ship and port, out of range of their comforting glow. We had two lamps for twelve people, which made it a little difficult to organise the evening so that everybody had something to do. Certainly everybody had an enjoyable ride in the lifeboat. Everybody was thoroughly dirty and not a little disillusioned about the sea bed, or the sea bed in Malaga harbour, at least. All that arranging and planning; all that eager expectation, and what did we bring up from down under time and time again? Thick, black mud that oozed its way over the sides, seats and floor of the boat.

In the dark we were not aware of how dirty it made everything until we had returned to the lights of the port. Consequently, inspired by the specimens from Plymouth, we still all longed to find some form of marine life amongst it all. We spent a full two hours looking through one dredge-net load of mud after another in the light of two flash lamps. One lamp was hastily used to flash at the approaching dark shadow of another boat that loomed up in the darkness, way above us, and gave us some inkling of our rather precarious position. The 'net' result of the evening's activity was a few starfish, crabs and worms. My report to the Malaga port authorities

1.   Mathematics and Navigation: Studies in school make the visit to
the bridge more memorable. (Page 60)

2. S.S. *Nevasa:* 'The next port Malta, was my favourite one. I loved the honey coloured buildings' (Student's extract). (Page 94)

3. Many local art forms can be seen in buildings, boats, carts, leatherware, pottery and the way in which food is displayed in shops. (Page 52)

4. Interview in Madeira for a Certificate of Secondary Education project.

5. Rubbings from the Acropolis for the School Resource Collection.
(Page 62)

regretfully stated that the harbour sea bed appeared to be too polluted to maintain much life. That was being diplomatic!

Our second trip out in the lifeboat was far more successful and even more eventful. We started from Tangier in beautiful late afternoon sunshine but finished in black night, not at all according to plan. We were returning to the ship after an extremely successful two hours of dredging the sea bed. We found sea urchins, starfish and crabs of every possible variety. We collected several jars of plankton. Then the unexpected happened. The lifeboat engine started to cough and splutter until it gave a final brave splutter and all was silent. We bobbed gently up and down, making no headway at all. Not to worry. Find the starting handle. No starting handle. No starting handle could be seen anywhere. It had been used when we set off; twenty pairs of disbelieving eyes looked. Could it have slipped overboard with one of the nets? The mystery remains unsolved to this day. All we knew was that the sun was going down, the wind was getting up and we were bobbing up a little higher and dropping down a little lower than we had fifteen minutes earlier. The officer called up the *Uganda* on the radio. The crackling began almost immediately. His voice rang out unanswered; silence enveloped us again.

The students were enjoying the adventure with their usual enthusiasm, but the adults were by now feeling a little out of our depth, beginning to wonder just what our fate would be.

There were, by now, white caps to the waves and for the first time on the voyage I was taking deep breaths and swallowing very rapidly to keep down the sickness. Darkness was falling, the wind was stronger and we were drifting towards the rocky coastline, when suddenly, rounding the headland, came a fleet of fishing boats. The officer grabbed his lamp and started to operate it on and off in the direction of the leading boat. We all strained our eyes eagerly and it was with great relief that we saw an answering light flashing to us and the leading boat changing course, swinging round in our direction. A rope was thrown from our boat to the Moroccan fishing vessel which towed us safely behind and twenty minutes later, into sight of the *Uganda*. Only then did some of the students realise how well founded our fears were – for a rescue boat was only just setting forth from the *Uganda* on its way to find us.

With this account the scene is set for a more detailed look at life on board.

7 ON BOARD

The situation whereby something in the region of 1,000 school-children from differing backgrounds, localities and age-groups are removed from their normal home and school environment and placed on board a ship is somewhat unique
A SENIOR STUDENT

DISEMBARKATION

'Embarkation usually takes place in the early afternoon.' Behind this matter of fact statement lies detailed and precise organisation on the part of all those responsible for getting the parties from their home base in an often remote part of the British Isles to the point of embarkation which may be a U.K. port such as Belfast, Clyde, Falmouth or Swansea or a European port like Leghorn, Venice or Ryeka.

In the first place on charter cruises B.I. has to take into particular account getting the ship to the nearest port for the Local Education Authority bearing in mind the economic viability of positioning the ship at one port rather than another and whether it is suitable from the point of view of navigation and handling passengers.

About one month before the ship is due in port the Company's local agent is instructed to make arrangements for the reception of the ship and handling of the passengers. These arrangements are complex and include the ordering of a Pilot, tugs and quayside personnel to berth, moor and provide gangways. The agent also arranges for fresh water to be supplied and ensures, with the fuel oil suppliers, the delivery of fuel oil. Arrangements must also be made for cabin passengers' baggage to be loaded on board or landed, for suitable areas to be reserved for cars and coaches and facilities organised for H.M. Customs, immigration and passenger checks to be made. It is no mean feat that in 1971 during 28 embarkations/disembarkations 5,947 independent cabin passengers, 27,040 students and 2041 Party Leaders were embarked and disembarked at U.K. ports.

When B.I. first made the turn rounds, in the early days, they frequently used trains and cross-Channel ferries to take the groups to the port of embarkation in Europe. It was thought that the train and cross-Channel trip would in itself be a valuable experience. On many occasions it turned out to be a feat of endurance particularly for those groups who had to travel from the North of England frequently with little heating in railway carriages and no fresh water. Eventually it was decided that air travel would be more satisfactory. This, in itself, is a more complex operation than embarkation at a U.K.

66

port. It involves the transfer by air of up to 2,770 passengers over two days in aircraft chartered from Dan-Air, British Caledonian, Laker, Lloyd International and S.A.M. using Boeing 707s, Comets, B.A.C. 1–11s and Caravelles with seating capacities ranging from 79 for some B.A.C. 1–11s to 188 in Boeing 707s. Aircraft berthing is complicated and on some occasions involves using six aircraft each day. Apart from the scheduling of aircraft, arrangements must be made at the terminal port for transport to the ship from the aircraft and vice versa, in Venice by water bus and coach and at other ports by coach. Venice does not always present the image immortalised by Canaletto. It is often fogbound, which means that if the ship cannot get into the Lagoon then the airlift has to be diverted. Fog is sometimes a hazard at both ends. If the airlift has started from the U.K. but the ship has been unable to berth, then passengers have to be found hotel accommodation in Venice at short notice.

If the planes are unable to take off from London due to fog, then it is sometimes necessary to find accommodation for the groups in London and B.I. have even been known to take potential plane loads of children to Brighton for the night. On these occasions an operation which normally takes two days has to be done in a single day. This may mean ferrying 2,000 people between Venice and the U.K. and the U.K. and Venice. Factors which add to the complications in this situation are that aeroplanes chartered for use the previous day may be booked for another charter on the next day when the fog has lifted.

Strikes sometimes affect the logistics. On one occasion the first busload of the in-coming party from the U.K. met a barricade on the causeway which joins the Italian mainland and Venice. The barricade had been put up by sympathisers of the waterbus men, who were on strike. It meant, in any case, there was no transport along the Grand Canal to connect the party with the waiting ship off the Riva degli Schiavone. The airport bus was turned back to Marco Polo Airport and instead of the complement of six arriving plane loads progressing in planned order towards the point of embarkation there was a pile-up in the relatively small airport lounge. The group of 1,000 children missed their aesthetic experience of proceeding down the length of the Grand Canal and were finally got away in a fleet of private motor boats across the Lagoon, in an operation completed half an hour before the ship was due to sail. But there were other lessons to be learnt and, as an eye-witness has suggested, the way in which Party Leaders and students responded to the situation was a credit to the British educational system!

At the risk of labouring this point, it needs little imagination to appreciate the effort and the energy sudden changes involve in the procedures for embarkation and disembarkation; anxiety, rarely shown, inevitably penetrates every part of the organisation, even the ship's kitchens. Coaches and special trains have to be diverted and particularly on the return journey a member of the Local Education

67

Authority contacted in case of emergency. If these problems overtake an Open Cruise there may be thirty different people who have to be contacted by B.I. headquarters in London who in turn spend many hours ringing up schools and parents. If delays occur on a Saturday or a Sunday this adds to the whole problem of communication.

Once a party is on board it is taken first to the dormitories and then to the muster station where it goes in the event of emergency; as one student was overheard to remark, 'The place where we stand when the ship goes down.' The Party Leader is then free to find his own cabin. After this, either before the ship sails or shortly afterwards, he and his party are called to the Assembly Hall for the introductory talk by the ship's education staff. This is followed by the first Emergency Stations Practice, the first Party Leaders' Conference and an informal party with the Headmaster and members of the ship's staff. Meanwhile the students will have had their evening meal, probably a familiar high tea of grilled sausages, tomatoes, chips, bread and jam, tea and fresh fruit to make them feel less distant from home. The key point about menus, after long experience, is that it is far better to stick to food the students know and like, leaving a less familiar cuisine for later gastronomic experiences.

Specimen menus include:

Breakfast
Fruit juice
Porridge, Sugar Puffs
Weetabix
Fried egg and bacon
Bread and butter, roll
Preserves
Tea, coffee

Breakfast
Tomato juice
Rolled oats, Weetabix
Ricicles
Scrambled egg and fried bread
Beans in tomato sauce
Bread and butter, roll
Preserves
Tea, coffee

Luncheon
Cream of onion soup
Roast beef and Yorkshire
  pudding
Carrots
Roast and mashed potatoes
Fruit salad and cream
Orangeade

Luncheon
Mock turtle soup
Salmon mayonnaise
Compressed beef
Bologna sausage
Fresh salad
Baked jacket potatoes
Coconut custard flan
Lemonade

High Tea
Veal, egg and tomato pie
Spaghetti Bolognaise
Creamed potatoes
Raspberry jelly and ice cream

High Tea
Green pea soup
Fried fillet of haddock
French fried potatoes
Swiss trifle

Bread, butter and jam
Tea, coffee

Supper
Biscuits
Tea, cocoa
Bovril, orangeade

Bread, butter and jam
Fresh fruit

Supper
Fruit cake
Tea, cocoa
Bovril, lemonade

THE FIRST EVENING

After the evening meal the students sample their first night's entertainment. This may be a dance, a sing-song, a feature film or quiz. The Fun Fair organised by the junior officers and school office assistants usually comes after the first forty-eight hours at sea and an 'eye witness account' is given later in this chapter.

By 21.30 hours, Party Leaders undertake one of the most important of their pastoral duties – ensuring that their students actually go to bed and settle down when they are called to their dormitories and do not merely transfer their social activities from one part of the ship to another! They will, in any event, want to see their students on this first night in order to cope with any problems and to brief them for the next day.

THE PARTY LEADER ON BOARD

It has been said, earlier, that the success of an educational cruise depends on the Party Leader. As a tribute to all those teachers who have taken this on, survived and returned to the task again, it is worth recording how a senior student sees their role on board. Because this account reveals that at least some of their charges are aware that this is no holiday for them; a fact in itself rewarding, and because the writer is still undeterred in his intention himself to be a teacher, it is hoped this will not put off the faint-hearted.

The Party Leader on his first cruise is faced with a totally new situation and has to shoulder new demands: he must find his way round the ship more quickly than his students and, in any case, students are guided round. He must accustom himself to new aspects of looking after his students from the moment they wake up to the moment they go to bed, and he must recognise his ultimate responsibility for them both in work *and play*; he must keep a close watch over his flock in a city that is probably totally alien to him, and be ready to deal with questions over passports and currency. He must understand and be able to interpret to his students the requirements of the ship's company. All this he must do, and do quickly. In short the teacher on his first cruise faces an 'abnormal' situation, and must shoulder practical responsibilities unusual to him as well as continue to teach in the 'normal way'. This new role may take a little time to get used to; for some, it may take a whole cruise, and this reduces the potential value of the cruise both for the teacher and his students. For many, there appears to be no help: 'Sir, will it be hot or cold tomorrow?' 'God only knows,' said an exasperated Party Leader. To which a voice from the back returned '. . . and he won't tell you, either.'

ORGANISATION AND TIMETABLE FOR A DAY AT SEA

For the individual student a day at sea may be as follows, but there will be many variations on the timetable and an immense amount of organisation behind this outline:

0700	Reveille
0730	First call for breakfast
0900	Morning assembly
0915	1st school period begins
1000	1st school period ends
1015	2nd school period begins
1100	2nd school period ends
1100	Party Leaders' coffee
1125	3rd school period begins
1210	3rd school period ends
1215	First call for midday meal
1400	4th school period begins
1445	4th school period ends
1500	5th school period begins
1545	5th school period ends
1600	Party Leaders' tea
1615	6th school period begins
1700	6th school period ends
1715	Voluntary activities period begins
1800	Voluntary activities period ends
1800	First call for evening meal
1915	Film
2015	Dance
2045	Supper begins
2130	Turn in ⎫ later for Seniors
2200	Lights out ⎭

The school party is the basic unit of the social and pastoral life of the ship and it is normal for each school party to be accompanied by Party Leaders in the ratio of one to fifteen. The entire cruise of say 900 students is organised into six groups of 150 students normally with 60 Party Leaders. This means that, depending on their size, there may be parties from a dozen schools within one group. The composition of a single group is illustrated by the example from the Kent Educational Cruise July 1971 shown in Table 3.

The six groups in total are important units in the ship's organisation; parties are called in groups over the loudspeaker for muster stations,

Table 3. Organisation of a cruise group: Kent Educational Cruise 1971

Group	School	Boys	Dormitory	Girls	Dormitory	Total	Classroom	Party Leader	Berth
A	Dartford Grammar School for Girls	–		30	18 Duncan 12 Fisher	30	Arnold	Miss B. M. Cope Mrs I. M. Markham	69B 69X
B	Dartford Technical High School for Boys	15	12 Tovey 3 Scott	–		15	Ruskin	Mr I. M. Smith	64Y
C	Dartford Technical High School for Girls	–		47	26 Benbow 21 Anson	47	Gibbon/ Hazlitt	Mrs F. L. Newman Mrs E. Tusan Miss W. A. Brearley	15X 77A 77X
D	Dartford, West Secondary School for Girls	–		15	9 Cochrane 6 Churchill	15	Rutherford	Miss C. E. Hyde	77B
E1	Gravesend School for Boys	15	Scott	–		15	Johnson	Mr V. J. Hills	125A
E2	Gravesend School for Girls	–		15	13 Cochrane 2 Cunningham	15	Johnson	Dr C. Agambar	121Y
F1	Northfleet School for Boys	15	6 Vian 9 Shackleton	–		15	Kipling	Mr R. E. Jones	73A
F2	Northfleet School for Girls	–		15	Dampier	15	Lamb	Mrs E. M. Turton	65A
G	Paddock Wood, Mascalls Secondary	8	Somerville	8	Beatty	16	Darwin	Mr K. G. Harvey	73B

cafeteria, deck games, lectures, lessons, and assembly. The day at sea is programmed morning and afternoon on the following pattern:

Period	Assembly Hall	Classrooms	Games	Private Study
1	Groups I, II	Groups III, IV	Group V	Group VI
2	Groups III, IV	Groups V, VI	Group I	Group II
3	Groups V, VI,	Groups I, II	Group III	Group IV

The detailed composition of the groups and decisions on whether there shall be group leaders in addition to Party Leaders is discussed at the preliminary meeting between the B.I. Education Staff and the cruise organisers which may be one or several Local Education Authorities or organisations. They take into account the particular wishes of the Authority and if there is more than one, the degree of integration one with another, and how to amalgamate small parties to make them more viable.

Where an Authority is particularly anxious to have a horizontal split for classroom work, i.e. to group students from different schools according to age, it is necessary to appoint a group leader to plan and supervise this part of the organisation and timetable, in addition to other duties which may be assigned to him.

In this case the hierarchy may be as follows:

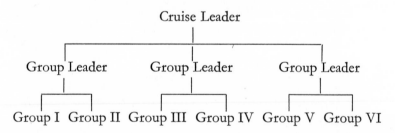

A great deal is heard nowadays about management in education and the importance of communication. It is, of course, a matter for each Local Education Authority to dispose their troops and determine the number of generals in their command. Decisions of this nature would provide an ideal simulation exercise for any education management course! At least one cruise organiser has had the courage to admit, 'we had fewer problems when we limited the people in charge'.

The school party as a unit works well for most of the activities; its members all know each other and if the party is a small one with only one or two Party Leaders, then the older students help with the organisation. There is a problem to be faced when organising the classroom work if the age and ability range of the party is too wide. If serious sequential work is to be attempted it may be difficult to cater for a classroom group which contains an upper sixth student at one end and a retarded reader of twelve at the other.

An alternative and one which has been seen to work well, is to form classes of at least similar ages from within the pair of groups which have classroom lessons together. As the pair of groups under the the Group Leader are in the classroom together, the organisation of the groups is the responsibility of the Group Leader. These classes are not of equal size as the classrooms differ. A typical scheme in Uganda under this system would look like this (classrooms named not numbered):

Groups I and II (330 students)

Austen	20 students	VI year
Burns	20	VI
Defoe	24	V
Dickens	22	V
Eliot	22	V
Forster	24	V
Goldsmith	24	IV
Greene	25	IV
Scott	24	IV
Shakespeare	24	IV
Sheridan	32	III
Stevenson	22	III
Swift	23	III
Thackeray	24	III

There are several advantages in this system, especially if teachers prefer to teach the level of work they most enjoy and feel confident to teach. It is sometimes possible for group and party leaders to plan a syllabus of work within this scheme which will follow the programme of lectures given by the education staff of the ship but, 'the best laid schemes o' mice an' men gang aft agley'. Political events or natural disasters make it necessary to reverse the itinerary or alter ports of call twenty-four hours before departure, with consequent strain on human adaptability and the most carefully prepared lessons.

A disadvantage of this system is that school parties are split up and not necessarily taught by their Party Leader. This may mean making special provision during a private study period for regular meetings which are essential for passing on to students all the information about shore visits and other activities and for conducting never ending series of financial transactions in connection with spending money in as many different currencies as there are ports of call.

Some Authorities do not attempt to group for classroom purposes other than by school parties. They believe that the organisation for an individual student is already complicated enough for the relatively short period involved, and they are not convinced that, from a purely teaching point of view, a division by ages is the most effective arrangement. There can be more difference in approach and in intelligence between two sixteen-year-olds from different schools than there is between a thirteen-year-old and a seventeen-year-old from the same school. They believe that to get an effective group it is necessary to consider educational experience and intelligence in addition to age, and this would make the business far too complicated and much too discriminating as between students. Moreover, better results are often achieved if teachers are free to use their own experience in the teaching of their own groups on board. Who is to say that a study in depth of the habits of the hoopoe is less educative than a quick scamper through all the glories that were Greece, before the ship docks at Piraeus? Moreover, follow-up work when the students return to their schools is often more satisfactory if the Party Leaders have been able to combine the writing of log books and the preparation of scrapbooks with their classroom work on board.

SHIP'S RULES AND SAFETY REGULATIONS

Rules and regulations are often considered to be irksome and unnecessary in the present climate of society; the instruments of pettifogging authority. On board and on shore, be it a question of avoiding a ship's fire or 'the undesirable attention of local youths', discipline can be seen to be essential. The B.I. rules sound formidable and unending but each rule is the result of long experience and each has been drawn up for a very good reason. They provide excellent material for discusssion groups before the cruise.

All Party Leaders and students should be fully conversant with the following standing orders before embarkation:

a. It is forbidden to sit or stand on the ship's rails or climb the superstructure.

b. Students must keep their feet on the deck at all times.

c. None of the ship's gear must be touched, particularly portholes and sprinkler heads.

d. Students must not put heavy paper cartons, apple cores or any other bulky objects into the lavatories, since this may cause serious blockage of clearance pipes.

e. Students must not run in the alleyways or on deck except during organised games.

f. The following areas are OUT OF BOUNDS to students:

   (i) All quarters occupied by the officers and crew.

   (ii) All cabin accommodation.

   (iii) The fo'c'sle head after sunset and when the ship is entering or leaving port.

   (iv) *At all times* the girls' dormitories are out of bounds to the boys and vice versa.

   (v) The dormitory areas between 0900 and 1200 hours.

   (vi) Any other area of the ship so signposted or notified by the ship's Headmaster.

g. Any person observing anybody falling over the side should shout loudly 'Man overboard', throw over the side the nearest lifebuoy and ensure that a ship's officer or Party Leader is informed immediately.

h. Any person discovering a FIRE, however small, should operate the nearest fire alarm and inform a member of the ship's staff or a Party Leader immediately.

j. The signal for EMERGENCY STATIONS is at least seven short blasts followed by one long blast on the ship's whistle, and a continuous ringing of the alarm bells throughout the ship. On hearing this signal all dormitory passengers will go quietly to their Muster Stations and will collect life-jackets from the correct lockers. They will fall in in ranks facing outboard and remain silent. Party Leaders will also collect lifejackets from the lockers, unless they are in the neighbourhood of their cabins, go to their muster stations and stand facing inboard with the parties whose numbers they must check.

k. A Party Leader told by a student of 'Man overboard' or 'Fire' should ensure that the student has taken the necessary action and then report at once to the Bridge.

l. General

All students are advised that:

(i) Transistor radios are forbidden.

(ii) Punctuality at all times is essential.

(iii) Tidiness in all the student accommodation is most important.

(iv) It is forbidden to throw anything over the side when in port. This practice is not only dangerous but regarded by the local people as a breach of good manners.

(v) The purchase of flick knives is prohibited, as is the purchase of knives with blades of 6" or longer; these objects are illegal in the United Kingdom.

(vi) Students who purchase knives, cigarette lighters, etc. ashore must hand these in to their Party Leaders for safe keeping until the end of the cruise.

(vii) Lost property must be handed in to the School Office where the owner may redeem it for a token sum.

(viii) Students are warned NOT to keep more than a small amount of money with them; the bulk of a student's pocket money should be lodged with Party Leaders.

(ix) It is strictly forbidden for students to bring any alcoholic drink aboard the ship.

(x) Experience has shown that in many countries, particularly in Southern Europe and Africa, the wearing of mini-skirts by our students provokes the local people and in some cases is regarded as an affront. The undesirable attention of local youths proves embarrassing both to Party Leaders and to students and it is therefore strongly recommended that mini-skirts should not be worn.

(xi) All students should be properly clothed in the cafeteria and common rooms.

(xii) Padlocks for dormitory lockers may be obtained at the School
Office on payment of a deposit, returnable at the end of the cruise.
Note: The following should be read in conjunction with paragraph (ix)
above:

'Although general Customs Regulations state that young people who have
reached the age of seventeen may bring into the United Kingdom certain
amounts of liquor and tobacco which may be regarded as free of duty, it is
necessary to point out to all concerned that the ship's regulations forbid
alcoholic liquor to be brought on board: equally no bottles are available for
students to purchase on the ship.

Moreover the charitable attitude of Her Majesty's Customs to passengers
from our school ships has been a notable feature of their return to the
United Kingdom during the past ten years. This attitude is one to be
welcomed but experience has shown that the possibility of abusing it might
lead to considerable inconvenience and delay to passengers when they
disembark.

It is therefore the practice that no dormitory passengers, whatever their
age, may disembark from the School Ships with alcoholic liquor. Arrangements can be made, however, for students who qualify to take cigarettes.'
m. Smoking

(i) Smoking is not permitted anywhere below decks, either in the dormitory area or in the Common Room and Reading Rooms. No students
may smoke until the rules are issued by the Ship's Headmaster after
consultation with Party Leaders.

(ii) Discarded cigarette ends and matches must be placed in the receptacles
provided on deck or in the scuppers. They must NOT be thrown overboard. A cigarette end flicked overboard can easily be blown into an
open porthole and cause fire.

STUDENT PARTICIPATION IN 'RULE MAKING'

In the Merchant Navy discipline and the presentation of rules and
regulations stem from traditions which are very different from ideas
and practices in many urban and rural schools in the mid-twentieth
century. It is, perhaps, unusual for rapidly maturing young people to
be startled by the powerful, uniformed voice of a Master-at-Arms
telling them, 'Whatever it is you are doing on B deck, DON'T DO IT.'
The response is equally startling!

It is tempting to embark on a discussion on the attitudes and
confusion which now exist in some educational circles – and not only
in education – towards the whole question of 'discipline', 'permissive-
ness', 'de-schooling' and student 'involvement'. It would be a difficult
task for B.I. to present these rules in a form which was equally
palatable to eleven-year-olds from open-plan middle schools; thirteen-year-old boys from public schools and coeducation sixth-formers.
Attitudes towards student participation in 'rule making' vary on both
sides of the Atlantic and, perhaps more dramatically, on both sides of
the Channel.

This may add yet another topic to the many which already appear on the agenda for pre-cruise preparation but only the Party Leaders will know how to discuss implementation with their particular groups. One approach is implicit in comments of an educationalist from across the Atlantic.

There are many educational values in the entire trip and not the least of these is the life on board – learning to sublimate personal desires for group requirements and to enforce them *together*. How can we use this 'good learning opportunity'?

1 *Evaluate present rules*

The rules and regulations are necessary and must be enforced – why?

2 *Theoretical solution or alternative*

(i) The goal of the experience is to maintain safety. To co-ordinate actions of the total group in the best interests of all and to provide a learning experience pertaining to the need for group discipline through self-discipline. This goal requires careful and consistent pursuance. Self-discipline and self-direction are required in this situation because 900–1000 students must operate from one base. Not every situation is capable of being 'policed' so there must be built-in group disciplines.

Self-discipline requires in-put in terms of a set of mutually understood EXPECTATIONS OF BEHAVIOUR (theory of expectations). The process of accomplishing this requires that the consumer is aware of and understands the goals and details.

(ii) It is required therefore to set down *positively* stated 'rules' which are differentiated and minimal for SAFETY, for SOCIAL ENJOYMENT and for EMERGENCY ACTIONS.

3 *Process of involvement through discussion*

For this a small booklet might be prepared for each group according to their needs, or on a wider basis, on 'How to Enjoy Your Life on Board' which could provide discussion questions – and suggested meeting formats – for use in advance of the group's arrival on board. These discussions would begin a process of *involvement* which could later be picked up again and consolidated by the Party Leaders.

Involvement leads to commitment and commitment leads to self-discipline and self-direction.

EDUCATIONAL RESOURCES ON BOARD

School-ship libraries[1]

There is a special reference library on the *Uganda* and *Nevasa* under the aegis of the Headmaster which is constantly kept up to date as new ports are added to the cruise itineraries. In addition there are libraries for students, cabin passengers and the ship's company. The libraries aboard *Uganda* and *Nevasa* are among the largest and finest afloat. They are maintained for B.I. at the Company's expense by the

1 This section is contributed by Dr Ronald Hope, O.B.E., Director of the Seafarers' Education Service and College of the Sea.

Seafarers' Education Service which acts as library authority to the Merchant Navy. The S.E.S. maintains libraries in more than 1,600 British ships; buys 1,000 new books a week and dispatches 350,000 books to sea each year. In addition, through its College of the Sea, and a unique system of honorary tutors (largely teachers including some who have been on cruises) it teaches merchant seafarers by correspondence. Shipping companies in the main meet the costs, although the service is partly dependent on voluntary gifts and also receives a small subsidy from the public purse.

The Education Staff, on board, call freely upon the whole resources of the Seafarers Education Service for help in their research work and for advice on the book prizes which are presented by the Captain at the end of each school cruise.

The main library for the students and the separate library for cabin passengers each have more than 1000 books. They are regularly inspected and refurbished by the librarian and his deputy from Mansbridge House, the headquarters of the Seafarers Education Service.

During the annual refit period all libraries are returned and completely overhauled. For particular cruises, or cruising in particular areas, special sets of books are brought and placed on board. Certain general principles are applicable to both the large libraries. The books have all been bought new for *Uganda* and *Nevasa*, and further new books are added as they are published, old and worn books being withdrawn. If a book is likely to be enjoyed or prove useful on a particular cruise it is bought, regardless of cost, and all the libraries contain many expensive and lavishly illustrated books.

The libraries for both students and cabin passengers contain every possible guidebook and reference book applicable to the cruise currently operating. If such a book is not on the shelves, it can only be that someone has borrowed it. Several copies of the most useful guidebooks and phrase-books are normally supplied. This criterion apart, the cabin passenger library is somewhat 'lighter' in tone and contains a good deal more recreational reading than does the library supplied for the students. Experience has shown that the students have neither the time nor the inclination for much light reading while they are on a school cruise. Their library, therefore, is a serious collection of books among which student and teacher can pursue investigation and research in any subject connected with the cruise, the ship and the places that are being visited.

So far as the students' library is concerned, the whole object is to make it 'the finest possible educational aid.' Teachers travelling with parties of students are invited to make themselves familiar with this library so that it can be fully used for project work. They may also want to use it themselves in preparing material for classes, and for noting the names of books that could be usefully added to the school library on their return home.

On each cruise, school parties nominate students suitable for election as library prefects, as well as ship's prefects. Needless to say the expense of running these libraries is not light and, alas, losses on some cruises have proved a significant part of the cost. For this there is only one remedy, 'always return a borrowed book'.

Educational equipment

In addition to the library, sets of mime and songbooks, records and art equipment may be borrowed from the School Office on board. Party Leaders are notified, in advance, of what is available.

The audio-visual equipment is in line with the current interest in educational technology and ranges from film strip and slide projectors, tape recorders and record players to an overhead projector and transparency maker. There is a dark room and photographic equipment and a map and information room.

Marine biology aids include a micro projector and rear projection screen, colour slides and a marine study box for the students' own experiments and research.

AN OUTLINE OF THE DAY AT SEA

To help the new school at sea settle down to a routine with the speed required by the shortage of time, a full timetable is arranged for the first complete day at sea. Students are woken at 0700 hours, and after breakfast there is an Assembly conducted by the ship's chaplains. Depending on the administrative group to which his party is allotted, a student may attend a lecture in the Assembly Hall, work in his own classroom, play deck games or engage in private study.

The Assembly Hall periods are for lectures by the ship's education staff on the ports to be visited and other relevant topics and they are usually supported by films and slides. In certain educational circles it is fashionable to condemn lectures as an old-fashioned method of imparting knowledge but the justification for the lecture depends on the lecturer. Whether he delivers it in the University Lecture Room, the school classroom, or the ship's Assembly Hall, if he simply regurgitates facts which can be read in a book, members of his audience are liable to fall back on their own resources, as might be suggested from a questionnaire in a student magazine which asked 'What do you do in a lecture?' The students were given the choice of answers '(a) listen carefully and take it all in; (b) go to sleep; (c) start necking in the back row with your boyfriend/girlfriend?'

In the meantime the first period is followed by a full Emergency Stations Practice and a Party Leaders' Conference and the timetable is resumed after a morning break with attendance in the Assembly Hall and in classrooms rotated with other activities throughout the day. Three more periods follow after lunch, finishing at 17.00 hours.

In 1960 when the British India Company first promoted the concept of an educational cruise in termtime, they had to satisfy Local Education Authorities and Heads that school work in the conventional sense could continue at sea, in order to remove potential opposition and suspicion that the enterprise was not a serious educational experience. Moving with the times, formal school work on board, previously identified with lessons ashore, has been substantially modified, although there is a legend that a classroom of boys spent an hour on the peculiarities of Latin grammar while cruising in the Baltic and there have been reports of unfortunate students battened below, glued to textbook illustrations of Greek temples, as the ship saluted Sounion. At the least periods in the ship's classrooms enable students to sit down. A group of students once estimated that the average pupil during the course of a voyage walked twenty-five miles on the ship alone, and climbed up or down 5,000 stairs! Classroom periods give an opportunity to continue the themes initiated in pre-cruise preparation and to collect and discuss material and ideas for the work which may be done on returning to school.

There are opportunities to discuss experiences and issues of current concern to the student as they arise; for example a topic from one entry in a student's log after a visit to Dakar where she had observed clusters of flies swarming on the faces of some of the inhabitants: 'I would very much like to live in Dakar and help all the poor people, especially the shoe-shine boys.' Or based on a comment from a sixth-form cruise to the West Indies: 'It is very broadening to visit other countries, it also makes it easier to see the problems faced by immigrants from the countries we visited, when they arrive in this country.' To a junior an equally serious topic for discussion: 'Sir, what is the difference between a porpoise and a dolphin?'

After 17.00 hours there is time for 'Voluntary Activities', when students with common interests such as photography, preparation for the end-of-cruise concert, philately or country dancing, gather together with volunteer Party Leaders to follow their own particular hobbies. Some students complete their log-books for the Captain's end-of-cruise prize-giving. It is not possible to re-create an impression of the careful study, collecting and presentation which goes into this, except by describing an outline of the not untypical log-book of a thirteen-year-old:

A STUDENT'S LOG-BOOK

A Poem   The Sea in Winter
Souvenirs of the Flight   Ticket; record of mileage; fork, spoons and packets of sugar, salt, pepper and powdered milk.
A Description of the Journey
Venice   The Doge's Palace. Postcards and cuttings from travel brochures collected beforehand. An Italian paper bag. 2 *vaporetto* tickets.
Corfu   Pressed wild flowers and leaves and grasses.
    Cuttings from Travel Brochure.
Cyprus   Orange Wrappers. Student's own description.
    Cuttings from Travel Brochures.

Jerusalem The student's on the spot sketches of The Pool of Bethesda and Pool of Siloam.

Her own copy of the Inscription in Greek, Hebrew and Latin 'Jesus of Nazareth, King of the Jews'.

An Israeli paper bag.

Athens Pentelic marble stones from the Acropolis.

On the spot sketches of columns from Olympian Zeus.

Sketch of the East Pediment of the Parthenon.

A plan of the Acropolis.

The horse's head from the chariot of Selene from the Parthenon.

An unfinished sketch of the Parthenon.

A plan of the Parthenon.

Pressed flowers.

After the evening meal various entertainments, dances, cinema shows, singing, debates, take place until the time for turn-in, which is 21.30 hours for the majority of students. Special privileges are arranged for sixth-form students, and a senior club meets each ev ening.

FUN FAIR

The social round gets under way with the Fun Fair and cabin passengers join in. An extract from the journal of a cabin passenger describes the event.

This mammoth affair comes as a relief after the first forty-eight hours at sea. The fear of the unfamiliar, the almost certain sea-sickness, is over; sea-legs are stiffening up. We are all set to go and go we do!

The cabin passenger, unless he is very alert, may well be unaware of what is going on aft. Once alerted, his curiosity will get the better of him and he will be unable to resist the muted throb beyond those doors which separate him from the dormitory passengers. As he passes through, the sound is explosive, all the fun of the fair is his for as long as he can stand the noise. The panatrope blares out nostalgic music, the crack of rifles, 'walk up, walk up', bowling for everything (if not for a pig), shies, side shows, fortune teller, rolling the penny, the lot, and over everything, the coloured lights and the uproar created by some 900 youngsters.

The almost impenetrable crowd in no way resembles the students who filed primly aboard in their school blazers. They wear such 'gear' as they have brought with them; jeans, the coloured shirts which may or may not conceal the midriff, the neckerchief. Later, this gear will be augmented with trophies bargained for at our various ports of call.

As our explorer battles his way round the show, losing his money at every throw, he may recognise a few faces among the villainous-looking stallholders. The Surgeon, in a gorblimey hat; the Purser in ragged T-shirt and scarlet 'sweat-rag'; the Staff Commander in clothes which beggar description; all showing their wares in the authentic accents of Bow. Our observer has the first indication that the ship's officers are not remote people controlling our immediate destination, but working beyond the line of duty for the success of the mission which is to mould the children and their teachers into an integrated whole, to create every two weeks or so a new school with new personnel. At this point, he may wonder how this excited crowd is to be controlled; he need have no fear, for ship-board disciplines have been well and truly absorbed; at 21.30 hours the music is switched off, the tannoy announces 'that's all for tonight, students' and they melt away to their dormitories, save for those who remain to tot up their takings (for Seamen's Charities, of course). Suddenly, the scene looks very tawdry, as the Indian deck-hands move in to dismantle everything. There will be no sign in the morning, as we look forward to the new day, and our first landfall, that this bustling fairground ever existed.

STUDENTS' CONCERT

Towards the end of the cruise there is a students' concert to which the cabin passengers are invited. Many students manage to bring musical instruments with them even from vast distances and remote places like Maynooth, Ontario; the collection ranges from the omnipresent guitar to the rare autoharp, and usually includes a strong wind section. Another cabin passenger was heard to express amazement that students were able to produce a programme like the following sample in so short a time, combining items from schools as far afield as Cheshire, London, Yorkshire and Ontario.

Students' Concert Programme

On the Banks of Ohio Standing in the need of prayer		Congleton Girls' School
Autoharp	Doug Glifford	Sir Robert Borden
Michael row the boat ashore This land is your land		Allerton High School
Sword Dance	Ruth McKernan Carol Cambridge	Prendergast Grammar School
The Ten Lepers		Prendergast Grammar School
Jack in the Box	Singer: Rowena Dale Dancers: Joan Brooks Ann Holman Lyn Passey	Congleton Girls' School Allerton High School
Ten Little Cruising Girls		Roundhay High School
Piano Solo	Lindsay Richards	Allerton High School
Raindrops Keep Falling on My Head		Band of Sir Robert Borden

Both Sides Now

'Uganda' Song   Rowena Dale   Congleton Girls' School
Please join in the Chorus
'Bring back, Oh bring back,
Oh bring back those moments to me, to me,
Bring back, Oh bring back,
Oh bring back those moments to me.

Piano accompaniment throughout by Lindsay Richards,
Allerton High School.

THE LAST DAY

On the last day activities on board end with several major events
including a Prize-giving and Carnival. Their impact on another cabin
passenger is described in the following entry from her diary.

Wednesday, 8th October 1969
   At 16.00, prize-giving in the Assembly Hall. Essay, logs, sketches, scrapbooks, tidiest dormitories and deck sports. Ship's Education Officers in
hoods and gowns; Captain dispensed prizes and made commendably short
speech . . . all over in half an hour. After this, there was an exhibition in the
Music Room of students' work, sketches in pencil, or water-colour, 'logs'
and journals, 'mobiles' and other art work, most of it very revealing and
some of it good; the important thing, to my mind, was the appreciation (at
least by those literate ones) of the strict discipline on board a ship. None of
these children have been subjected to it before; safety for this floating community in a hostile element is every man's concern, they may at any moment
have to accept 'No' from even the most junior of the ship's company, the
cadets, who organise the deck sports and club activities on board. These
young men wear contemporary gear for these activities, but are to be seen
in uniform for 'muster station' and for their formal duties. At a time when
everyone is falling over backwards in the effort of not giving any guidance
to the young, this experience is a hard one to many; it is up to the teachers
who accompany them to explain to those who have failed to understand
how a ship works and why this particular ship is different from trading
ships, because she is geared to children, etc., etc. Some of the teachers are
unaware also.
   On this final night, the Education Officer said, 'You must come aft for
Auld Lang Syne, it is an experience.' It was, and to me a rather frightening
one. Imagine over 900 young people jampacked in a confined space, jigging
to the noise from the blaring tannoy. 'Pray Heaven,' I said to myself as I
mounted a chair in order to get a better view, 'that they know how to
control this lot.' 'Should auld acquaintance' blared out; those on the outer
perimeter wept on one another's shoulders', the Lord only knows what was
going on in the middle.
   However, at the end, this solid mass just melted, poured away down the
companion-ways to their quarters below; astonishing. I learned afterwards

that the staff and teachers ringed this mass, like so many policemen, who at a given signal, moved into the centre, breaking it up.

Finally, one concludes that none of this would work were it not for the dedicated care of the staff, from the Commander downwards. The Education Officer, with his assistants, Matron with hers, the doctors and the nursing sisters, the Masters-at-Arms, and the officer cadets, all contributed to a 'spirit', a unity of purpose which we have not met before on ships. Some of this must have rubbed off on the children . . . it certainly rubbed off on some of the passengers. The Asian crew, with their innate good manners, were without criticism and their patience was unbounded.

THE DUKE OF EDINBURGH'S AWARD

It is possible for certain parts of the Duke of Edinburgh's Award scheme to be undertaken during an educational cruise. The preparation and supervision rests with the individual student and his or her Party Leader. Students over sixteen may count the cruise for the *Gold Award Residential Qualification* if they hold a special position on board, for example as a ship's prefect. It is possible to arrange some training particularly in map and compass work, in connection with the Expedition Section and to fulfil part of the work in the Interests Section with some of the following activities: architectural appreciation, photography, coastal navigation, ship recognition, meteorology, ornithology, folk music and stamp collecting. Since most of those taking part know well ahead where they are going, they are able to select their interest well in advance so that the cruise may provide the peak of their work for this section with possibly a final assessment being undertaken by an expert on board. With planning beforehand it is also possible to include some topics.

SIXTH-FORM CRUISES

Sixth-form cruises have been one of the special features of the B.I. educational programme since its inception. They have been organised independently by B.I. or under the sponsorship of the Commonwealth Institute and of the General Studies Association. The sixth-form cruises organised by B.I. itself have had a Hellenic flavour; designed to introduce students to the Mycenean Age, Periclean Athens and Roman civilisation. One Commonwealth Institute cruise was to West Africa and two were to the West Indies. The General Studies Association has taken part in cruises to the Baltic Sea in 1964, to the Mediterranean in 1966 and 1968 and to West Africa in 1970. Apart from the change in approach to both discipline and social life, one of the main features of sixth-form cruises, however organised, has been their invitation to distinguished guest lecturers, and the 'depth' of the academic studies.

Frequently these cruises have had an unexpected significance. When students on the Commonwealth Institute Cruise sailed to Ghana on the *Nevasa* in 1968 they were received at a Durbar by the African Paramount Chief, surrounded by sub-chiefs and thousands of his people. He made a speech of welcome in which he extolled the virtues of the British colonial servant, an unexpected gesture at a time when it was *de rigueur* to denigrate the British Commonwealth. Partly because West Indians are hardened to cruising ships, there was less spontaneity about the West Indian welcome the following cruise, and the long haul home across the Atlantic was something of an anticlimax. One practical result of these cruises has been the number of applications from former *Nevasa* students for Voluntary Service Overseas. The B.I. Senior Education Officer has noted that: 'The compassion of youth for the more unfortunate of mankind is, perhaps, one of the most striking phenomena of the postwar era and there is much evidence on many cruises that this is deeply felt.'

There is a roundness to the reflection that B.I. whose traditions were rooted in the British Empire over a century ago, is still contributing to the development of countries overseas even if this has taken a different direction!

GIRLS' PUBLIC DAY SCHOOL TRUST CENTENARY CRUISE: DAME KITTY ANDERSON

One example of special cruises outside the normal arrangements made with the L.E.A.s was the Girls' Public School Day Trust Centenary Cruise which took place in September 1972 and was unique in a number of ways. This was the year in which the Girls' Public Day School Trust celebrated its centenary; in June representatives from all the Trust's twenty-three schools had gathered together for a Service of Thanksgiving in Westminster Abbey. Apart from this central celebration individual schools planned activities of their own to mark this historic occasion. Miss Kellett, Headmistress of Birkenhead School, had the idea of a cruise with B.I. for the Birkenhead and Belvedere Schools in the Liverpool area. The idea escalated and in the end both the *Nevasa* and the *Uganda* were chartered for 1,500 girls, aged 9 to 18, from nineteen of the Trust schools. From Liverpool the *Uganda* sailed with girls from Belvedere, Birkenhead, Newcastle-upon-Tyne, Nottingham and Shrewsbury, and from Southampton sailed the *Nevasa* with girls from Bath, Brighton, Ipswich, Norwich, Portsmouth and from nine schools in or near London. Both ships were to visit France, Spain and Portugal – three currencies for the young to manage! Dame Kitty Anderson, Chairman of the Trust Council, went with the parties, sailing with the *Uganda* to Vigo and with the *Nevasa* from Vigo. She writes: 'The tremendous success of the cruises was due to the help of very many people who entered into the spirit of the occasion – to the ships' captains, officers, crew and educational staff and to the hard work of the Headmistresses and the members of the schools' staffs who accompanied the girls. The educational value of the enterprise seemed to me to lie in the exercise in community living and learning. For some girls it was their first experience of foreign travel. One little girl going down the gangway at La Pallice proudly announced as she set foot ashore, 'I'm abroad!' Girls from different parts of England got to know one another and compared notes, staff from the various schools met, and young and old mixed together. At Vigo where the two ships met, a memorable barbecue was held in the evening on Samil beach. There on the beach with the Trust flag flying, 1,500 girls and members of staff mingled with the ships' officers and educational staff and with the local population, who seemed undeterred by the invasion. After an exciting display of local dancing to the accompaniment of bagpipes, apparently invented in Spain, girls armed with large litter bags cleared the beach, and according to a local stall holder Samil beach had never before been so clean! When we returned to England and dispersed to our various schools to start a new term, one reflected that an ideal way for seafaring people to mark a hundred years of school achievement was to go on an educational adventure by ship.'

REFLECTIONS OF A GUEST LECTURER, SIR JOHN WOLFENDEN

Sixth Form classical cruise December 1971

The most abiding 'reflection' is sheer admiration. Perhaps a sixth-form cruise is easier to manage than some others – though I can imagine elements in it which might make it more difficult – but I can only say that the magnitude and complexity of the organisation involved are staggering. Start by being compelled to switch the departure point, at a few hours' notice, from Venice to Dubrovnik. Then mix together 900 sixth-formers, 200 'cabin passengers', the necessary number of party leaders, half-a-dozen terrified guest lecturers. Stir in the seasonable gaiety of Christmas. And the result is an educational and social experience which no single person present will ever forget.

This was a 'Classical' cruise – Delphi, Pylos, Athens, Epidauros, Mycenae, Santorini, Rome, Pisa, the lot. But only a small minority of the passengers were in classical sixth forms. This fact presented a fascinating challenge to the lecturers. How much do you assume they know? How can you say anything that is going to be of any interest to the specialist when the majority of the audience are not studying classics at all but history or science or modern languages? How much notice do you take of the cabin passengers sitting sedately in the back rows of the Assembly Hall? (Answer: none.) How do you escape boring yourself, and therefore your audience, when you are giving the same lecture for the third time? (Answer: it's never 'the same'.)

Everybody worked hard – the Captain, who never seemed to have a minute off duty but never seemed hurried or harassed; all the ship's officers and crew, who somehow had to run a ship with this vast number of extremely lively young people getting under their feet the whole time; the resident educational staff, with endless problems of timetabling; and, perhaps most of all, the party leaders, teaching and arranging and juggling with currency and generally 'keeping an eye on them'. And all this, mark you, over the Christmas holidays.

I suspect that some of the classics students were surprised to see what the mainland of Greece is really like. They had not imagined blazing heat at Delphi in December, or the superb perfection of the theatre at Epidauros, or the lowering height of Mycenae or the sensational impact of Santorini. Perhaps the non-classics, who had no picture in their minds beforehand, were less surprised. Certainly they were no less enthusiastic. And all of them enjoyed equally an impromptu football match with the local lads in the square at Pylos, the devastating public Quiz, the Carols, and the fancy dress revels.

Who gets most out of it? I am not sure that this is a very sensible question, because I guess that, as usual, each person gets out of it as much as he or she puts into it. It is, make no mistake, a serious educational activity. That does not mean that it is solemn or joyless – far from it. But there is solid work done in the classrooms (that, incidentally, is where guest lecturers really get put through it) and a day's programme which is pretty demanding, mentally and physically. A fortnight is quite long enough, at this pace. The fact that it all happens on a ship is by no means irrelevant. Life on a ship underlines the mutual dependence of everybody on everybody else, not just for enjoyment or comfort but for physical survival. Discipline there must therefore be. It is strict, but never obtrusive, simply because without it the whole operation would be impossible.

I would very gratefully take off my hat, if I had one, to all those who make this experience possible for these thousands of young people year by year. Certainly they provided me with one of the happiest fortnights I have ever spent.

8 VISITS ASHORE

My blood boils with interest
A STUDENT

DISEMBARKATION FOR SHORE VISITS

In a fourteen-day cruise there may be four or five ports of call depending on the route. A sixth-form classical cruise, for instance, includes visits to Itea (Delphi), Navarino (Pylos), Nauplia (Epidaurus, Mycenae and Old Corinth), Piraeus (Athens) and Naples (Rome and Pompeii). On some cruises the number of visits is limited to four; many L.E.A.s have reached the conclusion, after several years' experience, that too frequent shore excursions are a mistake and that four ports of call in fifteen days is about the right balance. One rural Authority has commented on the problem of city excursions such as a half-day visit to Athens which overwhelmed students who were entirely unused to a city environment. Here, possibly, the 'trial run' with a school visit to London or a major provincial port or city would be a helpful preparation.

Cruise fares include the cost of shore visits, except in a few cases where optional extra excursions are arranged. Half-day tours are usually organised, but full-day tours are arranged at some ports, e.g. Haifa (Jerusalem) and Izmir (Ephesus). Tours are accompanied by English-speaking guides and take in places of historical, geographical and contemporary interest.

The organisation of shore visits for 900 students and 300 cabin passengers involves the B.I. officers and education staff in an operation comparable to disembarking troops in the earlier days of British India's history. To understand what is involved is in itself an education.

Initially, excursions at each port of call are arranged by B.I. port agents, acting on basic requirements provided by Head Office. They submit excursion itineraries for approval. In the case of a new excursion a member of Head Office operational staff will visit the port and survey the route some time before the planned arrival of the ship and any adjustments will then be made. The emphasis on these tours is historical, geographical and cultural but more prosaic points have to be considered, particularly on full-day tours; comfort, refreshment stops and shopping time.

At least forty-eight hours before the ship's arrival at the port the

Purser informs the Agent by cable of the number of passengers undertaking the various tours at his port. The Agent organises the required number of coaches for school groups and independent cabin passengers. In most cases the Agent will cable back to the ship the coach allocation and seating capacities to enable the School Office Purser on board to publish in advance the schools' allocation to coaches.

To cope with the large numbers involved, tours are divided into different phases agreed in advance by Head Office and the agents concerned. These are notified by Head Office in the 'Letter of Instructions' to the ship. The most usual form of division is to have two equal phases one in the morning and one in the afternoon, but there are variations. There may be a one-phase operation, a three-phase or even a four-phase division. Phases are generally by equal numbers and it is decided in advance in which phase the cabin passengers will travel. Schools are advised in the Advance Information for the port concerned when they will be travelling and care is taken to see that no one school always travels in the morning or always in the afternoon. Division into phases may be straightforward or it may depend on the optional tours. Optional tours, booked and paid for on the ship several days in advance, are offered at the majority of ports. These may be in the morning or afternoon and obviously affect the timing of the standard tour for those concerned.

Cabin passengers and students are called to disembark over the tannoy system. At certain ports, where the ship is unable to berth alongside, disembarkation is carried out by ship's lifeboats. This requires careful attention to timing to allow the different phases to be allocated to certain boats, to gather on the quayside and move away without too much crowding.

When a full-day tour or a boating port is involved, packed lunches are provided by the ship and collected before disembarkation. Cabin passenger may have the option of returning on board for lunch at some boating ports.

The disembarkation of 1,200 people is frequently accomplished in less than an hour and such are the precautions taken to check the students' return that out of nearly 350,000 carried in eleven years only three have failed to be on board at sailing time; in each case this failure was deliberate on the part of the children who were eventually found by the local police and returned to the ship at its next port. A report is made to Head Office at the end of the cruise.

What may seem to be a smooth operation is not without hazard when, for example, returning coaches from Mycenae reached Piraeus after a tour to discover that the ship which was due to arrive from Nauplia at 18.00 hours was not there. Gale force winds prevented her sailing into harbour until the following day. Not only had a night's lodging for 1,200 passengers to be found in and around Athens without notice but they had to be collected from different points all over the city and taken on the scheduled tour of Athens the next day.

PARTY LEADERS' CONFERENCE BEFORE A PORT OF CALL

The importance of pre-cruise preparation for these visits has been discussed in Chapter 6. The B.I. Education staff give a great deal of help both in pre-cruise meetings with Party Leaders and at Party Leaders' meetings before visits ashore. They offer specific suggestions for preparatory study and ways of spending the period ashore devoted to independent sightseeing, because 'there is no more depressing experience than to see small groups of children wandering aimlessly about the shops of a foreign city, their money spent and their Party Leader out of sight, or perhaps to find bored and disconsolate groups, having a day in Lisbon for the first and last time in their lives, returning to the ship two hours before they need.'

Every opportunity is given for questions at the Party Leaders' Conference before a port of call. This is often an occasion on which the Chairman, the ship's Headmaster, has to exercise more than usual tact when, for example, having just given a detailed briefing on Ephesus and discussed the probability of Our Lady and St John having lived there, he is asked, 'Is Mary's house a café and will they be able to buy soft drinks?' Or, on bargaining in the Souk at Tunis is asked, 'Can the students barter for postage stamps?' Other questions may reflect real anxiety, 'Does the Casbah smell and is it really safe to take the children there?' 'What is the bathing like?' 'Isn't it a big risk to eat ashore?'

Such enquiries have to be taken a little more seriously than the remark made by a visitor to Crete who looked down on the site of the Minoan civilisation and exclaimed, 'Eee, we're a bit further on than *that* in Macclesfield!'

But however amusing in retrospect, it is a very real responsibility to have charge of fifteen girls in the Casbah at Tangier, or the supposedly 'bottom-pinching alleys' of Venice; to scramble on to a rush-hour train in the Moscow metro, when none of the party is able to read the name of the station where they are to get off; or to take a lively party round Funchal and bring the group back four hours later without having fallen too enthusiastically for the tempting glasses of Madeira wine offered as inducements to buy in many of the shops. The need for purposeful planning of independent sightseeing has been mentioned earlier and the Party Leader who recognises this will ease his task ashore. He will also be helped if the party contains a few reliable students to whom minor supervisory duties may be delegated: for example if he makes these students responsible for reporting the presence of each group of five it is easier than counting fifteen heads himself in the swirling crowds at the door of the Hermitage museum.

After the Party Leaders' Conference there follows a thorough briefing of their individual groups before the shore party sets out, and this is a typical student's checklist compiled by a thirteen-year-old girl.

EXTRACTS ON VISITS ASHORE

Students' checklist for shore visit
Check next day's timetable
See 'Tidy' Mark competition
N.B. our party letter is 'R'
Notebooks and pencils ⎫
Cameras ⎪
Envelopes ⎪
Warm coat ⎬ for CORFU
Rain coat ⎪
Rainhats ⎭
Meet on verandah on starboard side (right)
Wait until called
Must have a landing card
Go ashore in little boats. Have one free hand
Must not trail hand in water
Do *not* take a swimming costume
Go shopping to get souvenirs at Corfu
Drink *hot* things
Do not eat fruit without washing it or peeling it
Do not buy OUZO [a very intoxicating local aperitif]
Saturday
Write notes up on Corfu night but not about anything too much
Everybody to have an extra period on SAT. at about 4.15
Tonight
6.00 Monitresses go and get the sheet for the morning
Go to sleep early

Students' purchases
Part of the experience for which students save up, or are given by
parents sometimes considerable sums of money, is the invasion of
souks and souvenir shops. The following is an example of purchases
made on the student's first educational cruise:

Venice	1 onyx box
	1 glass animal
	1 key holder
	1 ring
	Postcards
Corfu	1 tile
	1 Greek bag
	1 egg cup
Cyprus	2 boxes turkish delight
	1 hat
	1 vase
	1 basket

Jerusalem 3 wooden animals
              2 wooden vases
              2 wooden paper knives
              1 cross and chain
              1 book mark
Galilee   Postcards
Athens   1 ring
              Postcards
              1 Greek bag
              1 statue

One of the more successful shore visits arranged by a party of grammar school students to Ajaccio has already been described. Months beforehand the students had written to people in Ajaccio for information about the island's education, industry, government and transport, etc. They studied everything of importance about the island and went with a lot of background information. They split into different groups when they arrived for the day and covered different aspects of life in some detail.

Visit to Leningrad: Chief Education Officer

Another example of the importance of careful planning is the special arrangements made by B.I. for visits to Leningrad.

It is usual for two or three Intourist guides, who speak fluent English and are trained teachers, to travel between the U.K. and Leningrad. They are available for visiting classrooms and to set up an Information Centre which can be seen by arrangement during the private study period on the timetable. This room – and another if there is a demand – is used for elementary language classes during the voluntary activity period.

While the ship's education staff normally give Assembly Hall lectures on the U.S.S.R., the Intourist guides may be invited to do so or to introduce documentary films.

Before the first disembarkation there are speeches of welcome from the quay in English by Russian students and British students reply in Russian. Final coaching for this is given on board.

During the stay in Leningrad it is traditional for a party of Russian students and some escorting teachers to be entertained on board. The guests contribute three or four items to a short concert which also includes contributions from the English students.

If a ship is in Leningrad overnight visits are arranged to the ballet, opera or circus.

A Chief Education Officer has commented on the importance of contact with children in other countries, with particular reference to the visit to Leningrad.

B.I. arranged for seventy to eighty pupils from the High School in Leningrad to come on board. It was obviously a laid on occasion and rather formal but once they were all on board the students took them round the ship and gave them a meal. Five different nationalities took part because on that cruise there were children of parents serving in Germany, including French, German and American. All of them and the Russians took part in a concert; the only way they could be distinguished was when they spoke.

The following day our students went round Leningrad accompanied by the Russian boys and girls; five Russian boys or girls in each coach. They made very real contact and gained new insights. I was talking with one of our students when he returned from the trip and he said he had been speaking to a Russian. The Russian boy had said, 'Have you got TV in your country?' 'Yes!' 'So have we.' 'By the way, do you ever have any programmes in your country to make you laugh?' 'No,' replied the Russian, 'we don't. Our programmes are only to make us think.'

The Russians took our students on the underground, went around with them and returned to the ship when we sailed. The Russian girls were in tears as we left. 'Come back again! Come back again!'

Informal visits are frequently possible when groups of students make their own way, meeting Party Leaders at certain times and in certain places. No doubt this puts a strain on Party Leaders but independent sightseeing and shopping excursions are among those most enjoyed and valued by students when 'they have a chance to look in the shops, listen to the people talking Greek or Turkish, finger worry-beads and smell the smells of foreign cities.'

A brief selection of reports and comments by Party Leaders, students and local inhabitants conveys the varied response of individuals to the organised and informal visits and tours.

Conversation in Corfu: Cabin Passenger
When the black-and-white funnel is offshore and a fleet of buses sets down the straw boaters, blazers and shoulder bags emblazoned MANCHESTER UNITED, what do the inhabitants of once colonial or mandatory territiories make of this new invasion? One cabin passenger on an early spring cruise, sitting by that curious relic of British rule the cricket pitch in Corfu, was asked, 'Do you belong to the children from the big white ship?'

The next question, slightly puzzled, 'Do schools in England have a holiday all the time?"

'No, this is a school ship with a thousand children on board and each time the ship comes to port there are different groups from different schools'

The Corfiot was doubtful. The British system of education was as strange as its sporting traditions. Hoping to floor the Anglo-Saxon: 'But how can it be a school, there are no classrooms?'

'Yes, there are classrooms on the lower decks.'

'Lessons?'

'Every day.'

Finally, as a real test of sanity, '*Please* then, will you tell me why your children are so white?'

Education is a two-way process.

Athens: Education Officer
'A group of sixth-formers went off on their own. Without any previous contact or arrangement they walked straight into a Greek school and found the headmaster talking good English. He invited them to spend the rest of the day in the school.'

Delphi: Headmaster
'The day at Delphi will remain an unforgettable moment in many young minds. Firstly, the unrivalled grandeur of the place. It began with pulling ashore in the ship's boats and then the little port of Itea with its friendly people. Then the bus drive – up two thousand feet to the great Temple ruins. Silver-green olive trees, thyme and cistus, asphodel and a hundred gay rock plants en route. Then the staggering height of the great ramparts which tower above the shrine and the vivid purples which splash the shadows of the chasms, eagles and vultures soaring overhead. The naturalists, who found little message in the ruins, identified upon a Doric column a rock nuthatch, which made their day.'

Malta: Student aged 15
'The next port, Malta, was my favourite one. I loved the honey-coloured buildings of Mdina and the beautiful Mosta church and Pro-Cathedral of St John at Valletta. The carvings, sculpture and tapestries were the most beautiful I had ever seen. I was especially delighted at the welcome we received as we disembarked. The button-hole carnations and four musicians playing made us feel immediately at home and everywhere the Maltese were eager to give us directions.'

A day in Madeira: Student aged 11
'We arrived in Funchal Harbour four hours too early, at fifteen hundred hours. There was a long concrete dock with three ships lined along it. The *Carmania* at the end, then the *Ancerville* and *Andes*. Between the *Ancerville* and *Andes* was a space of six hundred feet. The *Uganda* is five hundred and forty feet long, so that is where we were going to dock. All the ships were cruising ships. When we arrived back from our shopping the *Carmania* had left and the *Hanseatic*, another cruising ship had taken her place.

'All along the dock were street sellers trying to sell us souvenirs. We couldn't buy anything because we were too much in a hurry to get to the shops. Before we left the ship, a rowing boat overloaded with souvenirs rowed round the ship, trying to sell them. I felt rather sorry for them because we were told not to buy the souvenirs because they would be cheaper in the town.

'On the quay were lots of boxes and barrels. There were barrels of wine, bales of cane, boxes of bananas and oranges, sugar, onions and wood. These were all exports. The imports were tiles, pipes, and sacks of grain.

'The *Carmania* was a Cunard ship, the *Ancerville* is French, the *Andes*, the Royal Mail Line and the *Hanseatic* is German. The *Andes* was on her last trip then she would go to Belgium to be scrapped.

'In a little side street we shopped. All the shops were open to the street. I found that in every shop you could buy the same things. Any and all sorts of basketware, handmade dolls, leather purses, wallets, comb cases and cigarette boxes, wine, baskets, hats, hankies, head scarves, and so forth. Most of these things were hand made.

'All the streets in the town were cobbled and most in the country were as well. The houses looked very ancient and homely and the windows were very small but they looked as if they had been kept well.

'About the town were the well-known "Oxcarretas". They looked great fun so at the end of our tour our teacher let us have a ride. It cost ten new pence.

'The cars drove on the right side of the road. I saw more police than you would normally see in England. They were dressed in grey uniform with a grey cap. There were traffic lights as well. The pedestrian crossings were the same as in Corunna. Just dotted yellow lines where we could walk. The cars were British and foreign makes.

'I bought most of my presents in Madeira. I bought a pet basket for forty escudos and apron for Mum for forty. I bought a wooden cock for Grandad for thirty-five escudos, some Madeira wine for twenty-five and a wooden bag for twenty. The leather in Madeira was very good so I bought a purse for my brother and myself for twenty escudos each. The shopkeepers were very kind and they know you only have a limited amount of money so they put the prices down a bit. I bought everything at a bargain price.

'Also there were fruits. I recognised apricots and bananas. The bananas were two for one escudo.

'In the afternoon we went for a drive in the country. The crops, fruits and trees were plentiful. I couldn't see a bit of land that wasn't used. Although Madeira is hilly there are terraces all over the hills and every inch is used. There were some very strange and beautiful flowers. Some of them were cacti.

'The people were dressed in scruffy clothes and often I saw the children helping on their father's land. There were lots of children sitting on the road-side with grins on their faces waving to the coaches. I couldn't help waving back.'

An island of colour and contrast: Student aged 11
'A dark thick cloak encloses Madeira at night, a cloak of jewels, silent whispers, cold and lost like a child in a storm, like a beginning with no end. Dark, tall, fierce cliffs tower higher and higher until Madeira is lost and fitted into the night-time jigsaw.

'The rich, brightly lit casino the brightly coloured gardens of flowers the floodlights of the harbour, the dazzling lights of the sleepy town, all stand out among the jewels embroidered onto the dark cloak of Madeira at night.

'All's quiet, dawn comes, the birds softly sing a mysterious song.

The twinkling dew; the noisy flowing streams, a cool refreshing air. The sun wakes and slowly shows his head from the powder blue sky.

'The fishermen take their boats out to sea; the flower sellers take their place in the square, and the busy bustle of another day is about to start again.

'The waiting ships discharge their gift-hungry tourists into the streets of Funchal to invade and overrun the shops. The street traders hypnotize people into buying their goods. The children run about barefooted, whilst the bullocks ploddingly pull their brightly coloured carts around the jacaranda lined avenues.

'In the embroidery factories the women patiently create their works of art, a violent contrast to the smell and life of the fishmarkets, cafés and snarling taxis.

'An island of colour and contrast – that's Madeira.'

Madeira (Poem): Student aged 13
> A small island
> Very poor
> A volcano
> No beaches
> The mountainsides green
> With necessities
> And the people work hard
> Terraces have to be built
> Food planted
> Every inch must be saved
> To be used
> Bananas, oranges, lemons, sugar cane, vines
> To be planted
> To be bought
> Exported
> Sold
>
> And in the villages
> Poverty
> Thick reeking colours
> In the back streets
> Half naked children
> Playing on cold, stone cobbles
> Men and women
> With deformed feet
> Carrying heavy bundles
> Or leading staggering ponies
>
> Girls sewing
> Embroidery
> By the roadside
> Men
> Selling wares

To tourists
Or fishing
And mending nets

The island is clothed
In poverty and flowers
It adorns the waysides
Growing in towns
And villages
And the flowers brighten the windows and doorways
But the centre of the village
A church
Made intricately beautiful
With several altars
And painted walls and ceilings
Real jewels in the statues
Carved pews
And flowers
The church is the foundation
Of a village
People prefer
No money
And a beautiful church
'If a church is beautiful
Poverty
Can be overcome' the villages seem to say.

Less poetic but perceptive comments by older students, reflect some of the hazards encountered.

Ceuta: Student aged 15
'Ceuta was rather a disappointment to me. Owing to the amorous attention of the Ceutan boys we were not able to see many of the local places of interest. They made leisurely sight-seeing virtually impossible by trailing around with our party. But even so it was a thrill to see the flat-topped houses bleached white by the sun and the street salesmen, in their long robes and fezzes, that I'd read about in Geography.'

Freetown: Senior student
'After an immensely successful trip to Lumley Bay, Freetown, where everyone thankfully fell into the sea or sported themselves on the sandy beach, followed by a magnificent open-air display by the Sierra Leone National Dancers, the returning coach convoy was halted when the leading bus overheated and broke down on a narrow impassable road in the middle of nowhere. During the time that the bus cooled down and became workable again, the freed students had made a brief survey of the surrounding jungle-like countryside; one group had discovered a woman who, surprised by this sudden deluge

of unexpected visitors, proudly presented her extensive number of children, revealed her dwelling and pointed out her crop of what appeared to be pineapples which were her sole means of livelihood.'

Many educational cruises begin or end in Venice. The concluding extract from a Party Leader describes the scene and asks, 'What did they get out of all this?'

Venice: Party Leader
'The channel between Corfu and Albania is little more than a mile wide, so we saw the inhospitable shores and icy mountains of that land and later the coast of Yugoslavia before arriving, in brilliant morning sunshine, in the fascinating harbour of Venice. And here the children had a day and a half to ride about the canals, grand and not so grand, to poke through narrow alleys leading to little courtyards with enticing shops. Who wouldn't, for instance, look into the window of the Marco Polo Travel Agency? They clambered about the Cathedral of San Marco, were lifted to the top of the Campanile, wandered through the Doge's Palace, ate ices and drank lemonade in the Piazza. They took pictures of the Bridge of Sighs, gawked at acres of Bellinis and Titians and Tintorettos and Veroneses at the Accademia, and they fed the pigeons.

'What did they get out of all this? I suppose one could exaggerate the effects, but more likely, one would under-estimate them. Let me quote some sentences from an editorial in the *Cruise News*:

We are all aware of the professed purposes of these educational cruises to make us more keenly aware of the heritage of civilisation passed down to us by the Romans and the Greeks, to show us how other people live in other lands and to open our eyes to the world around us. As well as these aims, there has been an unwritten one which is just as important and that is that we should learn the importance of living tolerantly with other people, in the dormitories, the recreation rooms and so on. And we have learned a great deal about each other in the process and had a lot of fun at the same time.

9 THE WAY AHEAD

The strength of the British educational system is that for every devotee of a particular innovation there will also be a critic; a salutary situation which has helped to prevent the wholesale adoption of every new idea.

It would be unusual if, over the past eleven years, B.I. Educational Cruises had escaped adverse comment. Criticisms are helpful when taking into account the future because in most cases, if occasionally exaggerated, they are not without reason. They range from suggestions that educational cruises are a complete waste of time; sociologically unfair and selective because only those who can afford to pay or work for the cost are able to go; experiences are too overcrowded for students to make anything of it; 4,000 miles is too far to travel for four days on shore; shore visits are superficial; too many lessons deteriorate into money changing sessions; it is a strain on teachers and if the weather is bad and there is sea-sickness this is a further waste of time and effort; it is an unnecessary disruption of the school and a burden on those who are left behind; teachers go along for a free holiday; and, finally, it introduces the students to an unreal way of life – attitudes rooted in the Imperial past when Britannia still ruled the waves. On the other side of the coin, there are benefits which are implicit in this book. At least there should be no illusion that the teachers or Party Leaders have a care-free holiday.

A mere balance sheet of good and bad will not, however, provide the answer but rather suggest that the time has come for some serious research on the social and educational value of educational cruises within the broader concept of educational visits at home and abroad. Whether it is possible to measure the attitudes of pupils and to discover how they have changed for good or ill as a result of their experiences only those well practised in educational research can say but 34,000 pupils now travel on British India ships during termtime each year and research has been mounted in less conspicuous areas of educational activity.

One of the most important contributions B.I. Educational Cruises have made to school travel is an unexpected one. Their development in the last decade represents one of the first major steps in collaboration between a commercial undertaking and those engaged in the national system of education. Moreover it has encouraged the first significant move by L.E.A.s towards the direct organisation through Local Education Offices of educational activities outside the school and outside the country. Administrative staff who have 'cut their teeth' on the organisation of a B.I. educational cruise are now well qualified to take on schemes for international links planned by a growing number of Local Education Authorities as part of a deliberate policy to 'move into Europe'. In some areas they have appointed full-time advisers in this field. Nevertheless, freedom and flexibility have been preserved in the arrangements made by individual schools.

The social advantages were outlined in detail in Chapter 2 but it is worth emphasising that where secondary schoolchildren are drawn from their neighbourhood into large schools serving a wide area, real contact becomes more and more attenuated. There are other pressures such as homework and even TV which may reduce the chances of contact with each other out of school. For many, the B.I. Educational Cruise offers an experience for the first time of sharing their company with other young people in their age group for twelve or more hours a day, and often for the first time in their school lives they meet their teachers in a context other than the classroom. In the words of a sixth-form student:

One sees, among the students, the basis of a society be it a family, a school, a city or a country. There are those who complain but are apathetic, those who complain but act accordingly and obtain improvements, those who opt out of everything and those who have a hand in most things. Within two days of arrival on board the students who were effecting changes and leading all the committees were those who were pushing into queues and by the end of the week had become a sort of ruling class with almost impenetrable ranks. This for me was the most interesting experience, to see the development of a miniature society, as I see it in England, on board the ship, so quickly.

On the educational side much has already been written. A current description is that a B.I. Cruise represents a formidable example of audio-visual education based on live situations, language experience and visual images with an impact which the media of educational technology can support but not replace.

Be that as it may, there is a mass of experience and a firm basis on which to study future planning in consultation with teachers and administrators in the national system of education, independent schools, voluntary bodies and other commercial organisations to see how, against the historical background of the last decade, educational cruises fit into the general pattern.

THE EDUCATIONAL SCENE: JAMES PLATT

Fifty years ago the majority of British school pupils could expect no more in the way of travel than a once-a-year picnic outing. Since then, the five decades have given us the school camp of the 'twenties, the first real growth of visits to the Continent in the 'thirties, the evacuations of the war years (which included the first transatlantic school travel) and the slow but steady increase in visits and exchanges with west European countries in the late 'forties and the 'fifties.

Then came the 'sixties, the decade when school travel added a new dimension to British education: hundreds of school links were formed, and air travel began to overtake the sea routes to the Continent; British India revived an idea that can be traced back to 1913, and made the Mediterranean more familiar than Margate for 30,000 pupils a year; over 1200 sixth-formers attended a grand Easter language course in Paris; and a Welsh L.E.A. sent 800 pupils (it's now 1,100) on termtime skiing courses abroad – chartering trains, ships and even the London Tube for the journey.

These were the years when school exploring societies went beyond the old trails and on to Lapland, to the peaks of Greenland and Iceland, to the deserts of Iran. When field study and adventure centres were no longer just prestige items in private school brochures, but were bought by L.E.A.s as bases for training in outdoor activities in many parts of Britain. When school and youth orchestras went to play in Poland, the U.S.A., Canada, Bulgaria and Czechoslovakia. When school journeys grew faster than any sector of tourism other than air charter holidays in Spain. And when international links, visits and exchanges started to escape from the packaged tour formulas, and become the subject of detailed planning by L.E.A. staff, who began to give a formal structure to the pioneering work of many individual teachers.

The 'sixties were when school travel began to be democratic, when international experience as a planned part of school life began to move into the British school system. At the start of the 'seventies we have the most advanced school travel and exchange system in the world – if system is not too strong a word for a phenomenon of such haphazard growth. The very size and cost of this huge movement of pupils and teachers, much of it taking place during termtime, has finally persuaded many L.E.A.s to weigh one kind of school travel against another a little more critically. At the same time, some L.E.A.s have decided to take an active part themselves in designing and operating or controlling school travel projects, while others have set up links with school authorities abroad as a general framework for various kinds of exchange and study.

The best commercial agencies have responded by planning travel and study projects which tie in with curriculum studies, and by developing them in consultation with L.E.A. officers and teachers. They have nothing to fear for the future – quite the contrary. Other agencies which did so well in the boom years of school travel by offering programmes which suited the convenience and bank balance of the operator rather than the needs of pupil and school, face a more uncertain future.

The school cruises demonstrated the role L.E.A.s could play. Singly or in a kind of commercial partnership, authorities chartered the ships and themselves learned many a lesson along the way. We now have the first generation of L.E.A. specialists in school travel, some full-time appointments have already been made, and more are undoubtedly on the way.

The full-scale link with an authority in France, Germany, the U.S.A., Norway, Sweden or Czechoslovakia may be beyond the resources of some of the smaller L.E.A.s; we already have an eye to 1974 when negotiating new L.E.A. links. Links apart, a number of L.E.A.s have their own base abroad: a camp in Normandy, a youth centre in Dieppe, a mountain hostel in Norway, a *colonie de vacances* in Brittany. Others arrange exchanges with many youth organisations in Europe east and west. Some concentrate on sports or cultural exchanges; one has a team of 40 volunteers ready to undertake 6 week-aid projects from Holland to Labrador.

Clearly, a change has come over our system. What was so recently an affair for the children of better-off parents is slowly going into the curriculum for every boy and girl at school. And money is being found for it. This of course is what must happen, once the L.E.A. is directly involved. It may not be long before we have a democratic system of school travel and international experience, right across the country.[1]

Where now, where are we today? Which characteristics of the present situation should we build on, and which discard? . . . What to retain? Language courses abroad; a full term in a school in France or Germany; two terms or a full year in an American High School; one or two day visits, acclimatisation visits as it were to France, Belgium, the Netherlands; exchanges for half a term for half a class at a time; exchanges for a week, a fortnight, even a month at primary level; study and ski-courses in France and Austria; Easter visits with a week in school as part of exchanges with US High Schools; seminars at Sonnenberg; joint *colonies de vacances* with French children; joint cruises in the Mediterranean with Canadian pupils. . . . These are some examples of term-time travel as now sponsored by British Local Education Authorities and schools.[2]

B.I. will have a major part to play in facing these questions. There are perhaps three main areas for practical consideration; teachers' courses, educational technology and changing functions of educational cruises.

It is a rewarding experience to listen to hard-pressed Party Leaders at the end of a cruise when they are anxious about their students' contribution to the ship's concert, the collection of log-books and the logistics of disembarkation, discussing their ideas for 'next time'.

1 James Platt, Director of the Central Bureau for Educational Visits and Exchanges, *The Times Educational Supplement*, 24 November 1971.
2 James Platt, *Education*, 17 September 1971.

If in the last fifty years we have moved from the 'once-a-year picnic' to the situation described earlier in this chapter, it is not beyond the bounds of possibility that in the next twenty years what may now appear to be a pipe dream is overtaken by reality.

In addition to joining conferences on future planning of educational travel, many teachers would welcome in-service courses which might include the specific experience of B.I. Educational Cruises. Whether they were arranged on a local basis, as may already be the case or through other channels, it would not only give teachers a chance to discuss and hand on their ideas both on pre-cruise preparation and activities during the cruise but could also be an initiation for those for whom this is a new venture. Possibly some training programmes might be organised on board for teachers who will be taking over responsibilities as Group Leaders or Party Leaders in the future. Such a scheme would, it is suggested, help to ensure a continuing core of enthusiastic and skilled teachers in this field.

There is no lack of discussion, over the coffee cups, on the impact of 'educational technology' on educational cruises; the need to reappraise the function of lectures and to introduce up-to-date educational equipment and material. There are lessons to be learnt from experience nearer home which tend to suggest that some new ideas require careful sifting and an assessment of their value on grounds of educational benefit and cost. Others deserve further exploration not only by B.I. but by the Local Education Authorities and the schools concerned; the idea for example of producing sets of material including tapes, slides, charts, pictures and printed sheets each based on one of the main areas usually covered by the cruises; the Scandinavian Fjords, the Baltic, the Western and Eastern Mediterranean and the Atlantic. These sets might be built up by teachers and students from their own resource collections and could perhaps be circulated to other schools in the L.E.A. area from the Teachers' Centre or ultimately planned for distribution on a wider scale.

From the crystal-gazing generated at the end of a cruise there are two ideas which could have long-term significance, but for technical and economic reasons may be difficult to put into practice, although B.I. have already taken a lead on the first, namely the provision of more international cruises. As L.E.A.s establish major links with *Departements* in France and *Lander* in Germany there may be a demand for part of the interchange experience to take place on an educational cruise. Attempts to develop this in the past have not met with much success partly because of different attitudes within the educational systems of the European countries towards termtime travel and practical difficulties over dates for examinations and holidays. As links with Europe develop it is possible that some of these shadows on the horizon may disappear.

B.I. have already taken a lead on trans-Atlantic links. In 1971 2000 Canadian students flew to Europe to join their British counterparts on board. Some imaginative suggestions have included the idea of operating off the Eastern seaboard of North America leaving half the complement of British students in New York to stay with American families and embarking the equivalent number of American students to sail down the coast with the British students remaining on board. There are many possible permutations but, at at the end of the day, these schemes need to be cost effective and to meet the kind of development which the L.E.A.s and the schools require.

Perhaps less ambitious and capable of being linked with the existing pattern of cruises, is the idea that a period on board should be combined with a stay on shore to enable older students to get to grips with an archaeological, ecological or geographical field study. Theoretically it is possible to envisage several L.E.A.s combining to fly groups out to Crete or Cyprus for a week's field study to be picked up by a ship en route for Haifa or North Africa and their places being taken by another group whose cruise experience had come first.

One of the distinctions of the B.I. Educational Cruises in the past decade has been the readiness of the Company to enter into a partnership with Local Education Authorities and their schools; a partnership which has led them, wherever practical, to meet a changing situation. British India are ready to open a new chapter.

B.I. LOOKS FORWARD: JOHN SHARPE

Since 1914 B.I. has been a subsidiary of The Peninsular and Oriental Steam Navigation Company following the fusion of the two Companies under the Chairmanship of the 1st Earl of Inchcape, the B.I. Chairman at that time. B.I. continued under its own name to operate its large fleet of ships which flew its own house-flag and wore its traditional colour markings and insignia. The black funnel with two white bands became as familiar to British school-children as it did to people who lived in and around ports throughout Europe, Africa, India, Pakistan, Malaya, Australia, New Zealand and the Far East.

In October 1971 the 120 companies which made up the P. & O. Group, including many Shipping Lines, were reorganised into five operating divisions and the B.I. School Ships became an important part of the P. & O. Passenger Division, which operates the largest fleet of passenger ships in the world. In this way a new chapter in the story was opened. The School Ships are now supported by an even larger shore organisation and derive the benefits of flexibility and economy which such an organisation can provide. The constant process of refinement and development of method, accommodation and amenity continues whilst wider areas of operation are explored.

However, the essential character and atmosphere of the ships remains unchanged and they are manned by officers and ships' companies including education staff, who have now had many years' experience of this highly specialised operation.

There is no evidence to show that the benefits provided by Educational Cruises are any less valid today than when *Dunera* first sailed from Greenock in April 1961; indeed there is every reason to believe that there will be an increasing need for this type of experience among the young people of tomorrow, from both the national and international points of view. The raising of the school-leaving age and the reorganisation of county boundaries will generate new problems and new possibilities to which the service must and will be adapted.

From the inception of the scheme the Company has not claimed, nor enjoyed, the benefit of any form of subsidy from central or local Government Departments. In commercial terms the return on the immense capital employed has been marginal and each year has brought its problems of escalating costs of all those things a ship requires for her existence, namely crew, repairs, oil fuel and fresh water, port services, insurance, provisions, stores and equipment. In the ten years 1961 to 1971 the cost of the 'daily rate' increased by 100 per cent; this means board and wages of Ship's Company, stores other than victualling, repairs, maintenance, depreciation, insurance, etc., calculated on a daily basis. It does not include port dues but what is involved in merely keeping the ship afloat and ready to receive passengers. The increase in the cost of bunkers in the period 1969–71 was 155.43 per cent and in port costs 1969–70, 6.46 per cent.

It has always been the aim to keep dormitory fares at levels which are within the competence of the great majority of parents and families given a year or more's notice of a cruise, and this becomes more and more difficult in a period of rising costs when there is, at the same time, an absolute determination that standards of service will not be reduced in any way at all.

It is the firm intention of all those concerned with Educational Cruises that in the years to come the third generation of School Ships will follow their famous predecessors and sail proudly in the wake of *Dunera* and *Devonia* and of *Nevasa* and *Uganda*. They may be very different in technical aspects of construction and in their fitting out; there will doubtless be differences in the educational method, keeping in line with, and perhaps ahead of, developments in that field. Almost every week throughout the year a new comprehensive school will assemble at a terminal port at home or abroad and, if tradition counts for anything, will put to sea to the strains of 'A Life on the Ocean Wave' on the public address system, to be followed by Emergency Stations Practice, the Introductory Lecture and so on. With the active cooperation of its many friends so will continue into the future what Sir John Newsom described as 'one of the more significant practical developments of what, for want of a better word, I call educational experience'.[3]

3 John Sharpe, British India.

APPENDIX 1. MEMBERS OF THE ADVISORY COMMITTEE

MEMBER	REPRESENTING
E. H. Heelas General Inspector of Schools, Birmingham	
G. V. Cooke Director of Education for Lindsey, Lincolnshire	Society of Education Officers
J. Garne, M.C. Chief Education Officer for the City of Oxford	Society of Education Officers
N. McCorkindale Rector, Perth Academy, Perth	Headmasters' Association of Scotland
L. H. Porter Headmaster Bishops Cleeve Primary School, Cheltenham	National Union of Teachers
J. A. Stevenson Principal Teacher in Art, Preston Lodge High School, Prestonpans	Educational Institute of Scotland
Dr. F. Lincoln Ralphs Chief Education Officer, Norfolk	Association of Education Committees
A. B. Cameron, C.B.E. Director of Education, Dunbartonshire	Association of Directors of Education in Scotland
Miss B. F. M. Bland Headmistress, Ealing Grammar School, Acton, W.3	Joint Four
V. E. D. Haggard Headmaster, The Old Malthouse Preparatory School, Langton Matravers	I.A.P.S.

Dr Ronald Hope, O.B.E.
Director, Seafarers' Education Service
& College of the Sea

Mansel Williams
Chief Education Officer,
Caernarvonshire

Association of Chief Education
Officers in Wales and Mon-
mouthshire

A. M. S. Poole
Headmaster,
Marian Vian Junior School,
Beckenham

The National Association of
Schoolmasters

G. Fielden Hughes
Formerly Headmaster,
Queen's County Secondary School,
Wimbledon

Peter Millar
Formerly Chairman Protestant School
Boards of Greater Montreal

Chairman of Neworld Educational
Cruises Advisory Committee

I. Temple-Smith
Headmaster,
Whitleigh Primary School,
Plymouth

The National Association of
Head Teachers

B. H. McGowan
Headmaster,
Solihull School,
Warwickshire

Headmasters' Conference

Miss Wilma Harte
Under-Secretary,
Department of Education and Science

Department of Education and
Science

APPENDIX 2. CONSTITUTION OF THE BLANKSHIRE SCHOOLS EDUCATIONAL CRUISES COMMITTEE

Specimen constitution for a Schools Educational Cruise Committee which has been accepted by H. M. Inspector of Taxes 'to give exemption under Section 360 (0) (c) Income and Corporation Taxes Act 1970 in respect of any bank interest arising from investment of the funds'

1 The name of the Committee shall be The Blankshire Schools Educational Cruises Committee (hereinafter called 'the Committee').
2 The purpose of the Committee is to administer a Fund called The Blankshire Schools Educational Cruises Fund and the object of the said Fund is to supplement and advance the Education of Children attending Schools within the County, such object which now is or hereafter may be deemed by Law to be charitable.
3 The members of the Committee shall be the following persons:
4 The Committee shall meet not less than twice in each period of 12 months beginning the date of this constitution. The Chairman or the Secretary in his absence or four members of the Committee may call a meeting of the Committee giving at least 7 days notice to all members subject to Clause 15.
5 A quorum at a meeting shall be four and any resolution of the Committee shall be passed if supported by a majority of two-thirds of those members present and voting.
6 The Committee shall consist of not less than 10 members and not more than 15 members. At least one member will be an Officer of the Blankshire Education Authority. At least one member will be a Headteacher or a Deputy Headteacher of a Blankshire School. At least three members will be Assistant Teachers in Blankshire Schools who will be acting as Party Leaders for the cruises. The Committee shall be formed by
  (a) Members nominated by the Blankshire Education Department
  (b) Members nominated by schools sending the largest parties on the cruise
  (c) Members having a special knowledge of, or interest in, the cruises, and nominated by the Blankshire Education Authority or by the schools.
The normal period of service of a Committee Member will be two years to cover the time from the pre-planning stage of a particular cruise to the conclusion of the follow-up work subsequent to the cruise.
After two years, members of the Committeee may be re-nominated under (a), (b) or (c) above.
7 The Chairman and the Secretary of the Committee shall act as Honorary Treasurer, and shall be the signatories on behalf of the Committee.
8 The Committee's financial year shall run from the 6th April to the 5th April, and at least once every financial year the accounts of the Committee shall be submitted for consideration at a meeting of the Committee.
9 The income of the Fund shall be derived exclusively from payments made by or on behalf of children for whom places have been reserved on a cruise as

deposits or instalments towards the cost of the cruise, together with any income from interest which may accrue on the investment of the balance of the Fund.

10 The income of the Fund shall be invested in the Deposit Account of any National Bank, Trustee Savings Bank, or Building Society, as the Committee shall determine.

11 Payments made out of the Fund shall be made on demand to any Company or any other body with whom an agreement for a cruise has been made.

12 No payment for services shall be made from the Fund to any member of the Committee and incidental payments for administration expenses shall be kept to the minimum.

13 If the income of the Fund is being derived from simultaneous payments for two or more cruises, the payment for each cruise shall be kept in a separate account within the same Fund so that the interest earned on the payments for each cruise may be determined separately and used exclusively for the benefit of children taking part in that cruise.

14 All income of the Fund shall be expended on the said object of the Fund and in the event of any child who proposed to take part in the cruise withdrawing after contributions have been paid by or on behalf of that child, the Committee shall be entitled to repay the contributions, less any handling charge levied by the Company or other organisation or body providing the cruise, but no interest or other sums earned as a result of the investment of such contribution shall be payable to or on behalf of that child.

15 In the event of the Fund being dissolved, any contribution received from or on behalf of children who are deprived of the opportunity of taking part in a cruise towards the cost of which they have contributed, shall be returned, less any handling charge levied by the Company or other organisation or body providing the cruise, but without any interest or other sums earned as a result of the investment of such contribution. Subject to the return of such contributions, all income of the Fund not expended on the said object shall be applied to such other Educational charitable purposes for the benefit of children attending School in the County of Blankshire as the Committee shall decide.

16 The Committee may at any time be dissoved by a resolution supported by not less than two thirds of those present and voting at a meeting of the Committee, of which at least 14 days notice in writing shall have been sent to all members of the Committee.

17 Any amendment of this constitution shall receive the assent of not less than two thirds of the Members of the Committee present and voting at a meeting, provided that notice of any such amendment shall have been received by the Secretary in writing not less than 21 clear days before a meeting at which the amendment is to be brought forward. At least 14 clear days notice in writing of such meeting setting forth the terms of the amendment to be proposed shall be sent by the Secretary to each member of the Committee:

This Constitution was adopted at a meeting held on the   day of August One thousand nine hundred and seventy-one.

Signed:

Chairman:

Secretary:

BIBLIOGRAPHY

British India issue a bibliography of general books on navigation, astronomy, meteorology and travel guides.

The purpose of this bibliography is to show the range and variety of books and other materials for use in school, as a background to educational cruises. The titles have been listed under subject headings and in ascending age interest from nine upwards. Where appropriate the approximate age groups have been mentioned but Party Leaders will be the first to appreciate that reading ages and interests vary so widely it is hazardous to draw a dividing line. An educational cruise in itself represents a total experience. It is unwise to sub-divide the bibliography too precisely. There is bound to be overlapping and in some cases a lack of balance between different subjects and between fiction and non-fiction, but comfort is taken from the Plowden Report[1] for any shortcomings: 'There are simply books – to be used as and when they are needed'.

ART, ARCHITECTURE, CRAFTS

Age group 9–12
LEACROFT, H. and R. *Buildings of Ancient Greece*, Brockhampton, 1966.
LEACROFT, H. and R. *Buildings of Ancient Rome*, Brockhampton, 1969.
STEVENS, R. A. *Building in History*, Cassell, 1965.
FRY, JANE and MAXWELL. *Architecture for Children*, Allen & Unwin, 1944.
LINDSAY, JACK. *Leisure and Pleasure in Roman Egypt*, Muller, 1965.

Age group 12+
ARNOTT, P. D. *An Introduction to Greek Theatre*, Macmillan, 1959.
HARRIS, H. A. *Greek Athletes and Athletics*, Hutchinson, 1964.
SNODGRASS, A. M. *Arms and Armour of the Greeks*, Thames and Hudson, 1967.
DUNCAN, A. *The Noble Sanctuary – Portrait of a Holy Place in Arab Jerusalem*, Longman, 1972.
HOUSTON, MARY G. *Ancient Greek, Roman and Byzantine Costume and Decoration*, A. and C. Black, 1963.
CROOK, J. M. *The British Museum*, Allen Lane, The Penguin Press, 1972.
HIGGINS, R. *Minoan and Mycenaean Art*, Thames and Hudson, 1967.
WYCHERLEY, R. E. *How the Greeks Built Cities*, Macmillan, 1967.
MANSBRIDGE, J. *Graphic History of Architecture*, Batsford, 1967.
STRONG, D. E. *The Classical World*, Hamlyn, 1967.
BARRON, J. *Greek Sculpture*, Studio Vista, 1965.
BOARDMAN, J. *Greek Art*, Thames and Hudson, 1964.
MINGAZZINI, P. *Greek Pottery Painting*, Hamlyn, 1969.

1 Plowden Report: 'Children and their Primary Schools'. A report of the Central Advisory Council for Education (England) under the Chairmanship of Lady Plowden, October 1966.

MORTIMER WHEELER, R. E. *Roman Art and Architecture,* Thames and Hudson, 1964.

The Story of Sculpture, Marshall Cavendish, 1969.

The Story of Architecture, Marshall Cavendish, 1969.

BROWN, F. E. *Roman Architecture,* Studio Vista, 1968.

HILL, D. and GRABAR, O. *Islamic Architecture and Decoration,* Faber, 1965.

PLOMMER, H. (Ed.). *Ancient and Classical Architecture* (Simpson's *History of Architectural Development* for advanced students), Longmans, 1956.

Visual Aids

Educational Productions Limited: filmstrips
 Art Through the Ages
  (A series of 10 filmstrips in colour covering the history of art from
  A.D. 950 to the present day.)

Let's Visit the Museum	B/W
History of Pattern. Part 1	B/W

  (Decorative art through the periods of the Savage Tribes, Egyptians,
  Assyrians, Greeks and Romans.)

History of Pattern. Part 2	B/W

  (Decorative art through the Pompeian, Byzantine, Turkish and
  Mooresque periods.)

5,000 Years of Egyptian Art	Col.
Religious Art	B/W
European Architecture	Col.

  (A brief survey – Greek temples to St Paul's cathedral – spanning
  2,500 years. In collaboration with Thames and Hudson.)

Educational Productions Limited. Unesco Slidesets

Egypt: Paintings from Tombs and Temples	Col.
Yugoslavian Mediaeval Frescoes	Col.
Spain: Romanesque Paintings	Col.
Cyprus: Byzantine Mosaics and Frescoes	Col.
Israel: Ancient Mosaics	Col.
U.S.S.R. Early Russian Ikons	Col.

Encyclopaedia Britannica coloured prints
 Historical Reconstruction of Rome
 Historical Reconstruction of Ancient Greece
 Historical Reconstruction of Pompeii

Educational Productions Limited: Wallcharts
 History of Style
 History of Western Art

Gateway: Filmstrips/Slides

Ancient Athens	Col.
Acropolis	Col.
Ancient Rome	Col.
Pompeii	Col.

Visual Publications: filmstrips
 Architecture

The Elements of Architecture	B/W

   Greek
   Roman

Early Christian and Byzantine	B/W

   Romanesque
   Gothic
   Renaissance and Baroque

  Greek Art

Cycladic and Minoan	Col.

Mycenaean to Early Archaic	Col.
Archaic Period	Col.
Greece and Magna Craecia	Col.
Hellenistic Period	Col.
The Etruscans	Col.
History of the European theatre	
Greek Theatre	Col.
Roman Theatre	Col.
Roman art	
City and Temple	Col.
Arch and Theatre	Col.
Structures	Col.
Pompeii	Col.
Sculpture, Painting and Mosaic	Col.

ASTRONOMY

Age group 9–12
BRUCK, M. T. *The Night Sky*, Ladybird, 1965.
WORVILL, R. *Exploring Space*, Ladybird, 1970.
STEPHENSON, G. *Read About Science: Stars and Planets Galaxies*, Longmans, 1966.
MOORE, P. *Stars and Space*, Black, 1966.
OWEN, E. and GEMELL, I. *The Night Sky*, Blackwell, 1965.

Age group 12–16
MOORE, P. *The Stars* (Young Scientist Series), Weidenfeld & Nicholson, 1962.
WORVILLE, R. *Sky and Stars*, Ward Lock, 1965
MOORE, P. *The Observer's Book of Astronomy*, Warne, 1962.
WENHAM, E. J. *Planetary Astronomy*, Longman, 1969.
RONAN, D. (Ed.). *The Discovery of the Galaxies*, Jackdaw, 1967.
DIETZ, D. *All About the Universe*, W. H. Allen, 1966.

Age group 16–18
SMART, W. M. *The Riddle of the Universe*, Longmans, 1968.
MOORE, P. *Basic Astronomy*, Oliver and Boyd, 1967.
MOORE, P. *The Development of Astronomical Thought*, Oliver and Boyd, 1969.

Visual Aids
Maps, posters and transparencies available from London Planetarium
Educational Productions Limited: filmstrips

Astronomy	B/W
The Solar System	Col.

Encyclopaedia Britannica filmstrips

The Earth and its Neighbours in Space	Col.

Encyclopaedia Britannica coloured prints

The Solar System	B/W
Scanning the Universe	B/W

EARTH, AIR AND WATER

Age group 9–12
LOVITT, D. *Fish From the Sea*, Blackwood, 1963.
LOVITT, D. *The Weather and the Earth* (Science on the March series, No. 3), Longmans, 1954.
VEVERS, G. *Life in the Sea*, Bodley Head, 1963.
VEVERS, G. *The Seashore and Seashore Life*, Ladybird, 1964.

VEVERS, G. *Sea and Estuary Birds*, Ladybird, 1967.
NEWING, F. E. and BOEWOOD, R. *Weather*, Ladybird, 1962.
EYRE, W. *Mountains and Volcanoes* (Let's Look at our Planet Series), Chapman, 1969.
BARKER, R. S. *The Study Book of Weather*, Bodley Head, 1962.
CRAIG, G. *This Restless Earth*, Oliver and Boyd, 1962.

Age group 12–16
NIGHTINGALE, C. *Exploiting the Oceans*, Methuen, 1968.
ALEXANDER, M. *Behind the Scenes with a Fishing Fleet*, Dent, 1965.
ALLISON, I. *Deep-Sea Fishermen*, Ward Lock, 1961.
JEFFERIES, G. (Ed.). *Volcanoes*, Jackdaw, 1969.
CALDER, N. *The Restless Earth*, B.B.C. Publications, 1972.
SCORER, R. S. and WEXLER, H. *A Colour Guide to Clouds*, Pergamon Press, 1963.
KEELING, C. H. *Meet the Birds*, Harrap, 1968.
WELLMAN, A. *Earthquakes and Volcanoes*, Weidenfeld & Nicholson, 1962.
DUDLEY STAMP, L. *The Earth's Crust*, Harrap, 1951.
EVANS, I. O. *The Observer's Book of Geology*, Warne, 1971.

Age group 12–16
SCHOPFER S. *The Young Specialist Looks at Weather*, Burke, 1963.
LESTER, R. M. *The Observer's Book of Weather*, Warne, 1955.
PETRIE, J. *The Earth*, Oxford Univ. Press, 1967.
LE DANOIS, E. *Marine Life of Coastal Waters*, Harrap, 1957.
ENGEL, L. and Editors of *Life. The Sea*, Time Life, 1968.
CHANDLER, T. J. *Modern Meteorology and Climatology*, Nelson, 1972.

Age group 16–18
The Face of the World, Marshall Cavendish, 1969.
HOLMES, A. *Principles of Physical Geology*, Nelson, 1965.
EARL and PETER. *Maritime Meteorology*, Maritime Press, 1968.
HUXLEY, Anthony (Ed.). *Standard Encyclopaedia of the World's Oceans and Islands*, Weidenfeld and Nicholson, 1963.

Visual aids
Longman
 Nuffield Secondary Science filmloops:
  Volcanoes Col.
 Longman loops: Geography Col.
  1. The Heat Budget of the Earth and the Atmosphere
  2. The Development of Sea Breezes
  3. The Origin and Characteristics of Föhn Winds
  4. The Formation of Surface High and Low Pressure Systems
  5. The Formation of Rain
  6. Hail Formation in a Severe Storm
  7. The Weather Associated with a Warm Front
  8. The Weather Associated with a Cold Front
Common Ground filmstrips
 The Weather Map Col.
 Volcanoes B/W
Encyclopaedia Britannica filmstrips
 Investigating Rock Series Col.
 The Earth and its Wonders Series: The Story of Volcanoes Col.
Encyclopaedia Britannica coloured prints:
 Oceanography: Understanding our Deep Frontier
 Volcanoes
 The Sea
 Earth Movements

Educational Productions Limited: filmstrips
  Volcanoes   B/W
  Geology of Sea and Lakes   B/W
Visual Publications filmstrips
  The Origins of the Earth
    Fold Mountains   Col.
      Volcanoes I
      Volcanoes II
    The Sea I: erosion   Col.
    The Sea II: deposition   Col.

FICTION
Age group 9–12
RENAULT, M. *The Lion in the Gateway* (ancient Greece), Longmans, 1964.
TREECE, H. *The Windswept City* (Troy), Hamish Hamilton, 1967.
TREECE, H. *Viking's Dawn*, Penguin, 1967.
SHARWOOD SMITH. *Modern Stories of Ancient Greece*, Longman, 1969.

Age group 12–16
HOPE-SIMPSON, J. *The Unknown Island* (ancient Sicily), Hamish Hamilton, 1968.
TREASE, G. *The Crown of Violet* (ancient Greece), Penguin, 1968.
GREEN, R. L. *The Land Beyond the North* (ancient Greece), Bodley Head, 1958.
GREEN, R. L. *The Luck of Troy*, Penguin, 1967.
HOUSEHOLD, G. *Xenophon's Adventure* (ancient Greece), Bodley Head, 1961.
RAY, M. *The Standing Lions* (ancient Greece), Faber, 1968.
RAY, M. *The Voice of Apollo* (ancient Greece), Jonathan Cape, 1964.
WARNER, R. *Greeks and Trojans*, Heinemann, 1952.
WARNER, R. *Athens at War*, Bodley Head, 1970.
WARNER, R. *Pericles the Athenian*, Collins, 1963.
MCLEISH, K. *Land of the Eagles* (ancient Rome), Longman, 1969.
BAUMANN, H. *I Marched with Hannibal* (ancient Rome), Oxford Univ. Press, 1961.
SPEARE, E. G. *The Bronze Bow* (ancient Rome), Penguin, 1964.
KER WILSON, B. *Beloved of the Gods*, Longmans, 1965.
HENTY, G. A. *The Young Carthaginian*, Dragon Books, 1967.
TREASE, G. *Follow my Black Plume* (Italy-risorgimento), Macmillan, 1963.
TREASE, G. *A Thousand for Sicily* (Italy-risorgimento), Macmillan, 1964.
WELCH, R. *Knight Crusader*, Oxford Univ. Press, 1970.

Age group 16–18
RENAULT, M. *The King Must Die* (ancient Greece), Longmans, 1966.
RENAULT, M. *The Bull from the Sea* (ancient Greece), Longmans, 1964.
RENAULT, M. *The Mask of Apollo* (ancient Greece), Longmans, 1966.
GRAVES, R. *I, Claudius* (Rome), Penguin, 1969.
GRAVES, R. *Claudius the God* (Rome), Penguin, 1970.

GEOGRAPHY
Age group 9–12
MEAD, M. *People and Places*, Blackie, 1964.
SASEK, M. *This is Israel*, W. H. Allen, 1962.
SASEK, M. *This is Venice*, W. H. Allen, 1961
PAPAS, W. *A Letter from Israel*, Oxford Univ. Press, 1968.
SHERIDAN, I. *We go to Norway and Sweden*, Harrap, 1965.
DUNN, M. *We go to Denmark*, Harrap, 1960.
GADSBY, J. and D. *Looking at the World*, A. & C. Black, 1964.

Age group 12–16
CLAYTON, R. and MILES, J. *Scandinavia* (Finding Out Books), Weidenfeld and Nicholson, 1967.

TILLYARD, A. *The Land and People of Yugoslavia*, A. & C. Black, 1963.
MARTIN, R. *The Land and People of Spain*, A. & C. Black, 1961.
MARTIN, R. *The Land and People of Italy*, A. & C. Black, 1961.
HUXLEY, F. *Peoples of the World in Colour*, Blandford, 1964.
CASH, A. *Great Neighbours: U.S.S.R.*, Ward Lock, 1965.
GIANAKOULIS, T. *Greece and her People*, Lutterworth, 1958.
PEMBERTON, P. H. *Neighbours in Europe*, Ward Lock, 1967.
LAWRENCE, J. *Soviet Russia*, Benn, 1967.
MILLER, H. *The Colossus of Maroussi*, Penguin, 1963.

Age group 16–18
KERR, J. *Western Europe: A Modern Study*, Chambers, 1966.
WALKER, D. S. *The Mediterranean Lands*, Methuen, 1965.
MONKHOUSE, F. J. *Principles of Physical Geography*, U.L.P., 1970.
HOUSTON, J. M. *The Western Mediterranean World*, Longmans, 1964.
MILLWARD, R. *Scandinavian Lands*, Macmillan, 1964.

Visual aids

Common Ground filmstrips

Italy	B/W
Life Among the Arabs	Col.
Life on a Kibbutz	Col.
A Norwegian Fjord	Col.
Morocco	Col.
Mediterranean Climatic Regions	B/W
Israel, Introduction to	Col.
Spain, Introduction to	Col.
Denmark, Introduction to	Col.
The Netherlands Delta Project	Col.
The Reclamation of the Zyder Zee	Col.
A Journey Down the Nile	Col.
Across the Yugoslav Karst	Col.
Italy: The Changing South	Col.
Berbers of the Atlas Mountains	Col.

Educational Productions Limited: filmstrips

Everyday Life in

Spain	Col.
Gibraltar	Col.
Italy	Col.
Netherlands	Col.
W. Norway	Col.
Greece	Col.
Cyprus	Col.
Syria and Lebanon	Col.
Iceland – General Survey	Col.
Iceland – Fishing Industry	Col.
Mediterranean Harvests	Col.
Northern Italy	Col.
Central and Southern Italy	Col.
Spain	Col.
Norway	Col.
Sweden	Col.
Denmark	Col.
The Netherlands	Col.
Russia	Col.
Portugal	Col.

Longman filmstrips
Life in Spain   Col.
Visual Publications filmstrips
The Earth Today
Spain   Col.
    I Atlantic Spain
    II Mediterranean Spain
    III The Tablelands
Italy   Col.
    I Continental Italy
    II Central Italy
    III The Islands

HISTORY (GENERAL)

Age group 9–12
BARTLETT THOMPSON, E. *Africa Past and Present*, Longman Young Books, 1968.
PROCTOR, G. L. *The Vikings*, Longmans, 1959.
BAILEY, V. and WISE, E. *The Crusades* (Focus on History No. 6), Longman, 1969.
RICH, L. D. *The First Book of Vikings*, Ward, 1963.
TREECE, H. *Know About the Crusades*, Blackie, 1963.
BELL, G. C. *The Crusades*, E. J. Arnold, 1966.
DUVOISIN, R. *They Put Out to Sea*, U.L.P., 1959
HOBLEY, L. F. *Early Explorers* (to A.D. 1500), Methuen, 1961.
LOBBAN, R. D. *The Crusades*, U.L.P., 1966.

Age group 12–16
JONES, D. *The Arab World*, Hamish Hamilton, 1966.
WALKER, K. S. *Saladin, Sultan of the Holy Sword*, Dobson, 1971.
ROUTH, C. R. N. *They Saw it Happen in Europe 1450–1600*, Blackwell, 1965.
WENZEL, M. *Finding out about the Byzantines* (Exploring the Past Series), Muller, 1965.
BULL, G. *The Renaissance*, Weidenfeld & Nicholson, 1968.
SELLMAN, R. R. *The Crusades*, Methuen, 1964.
WILLIAMS, J. *Knights of the Crusades*, Cassel Caravel, 1963.
DONOVAN, F. R. *The Vikings*, Cassel Caravel, 1965.
MOSCOW, H. *Russia Under the Czars*, Cassel Caravel, 1964.
HALLIDAY, E. M. *Russia in Revolution*, Cassel Caravel, 1968.
HASLER, J. *The Making of Russia*, Longman, 1969.
SIMPSON, J. *Everyday Life in the Viking Age*, Batsford, 1967.
DAVIDSON, B. and BUAH, F. K. *The Growth of African Civilisation* (A history of W. Africa), Longmans, 1965.
RICHARDSON, P. *The Expansion of Europe 1400–1660*, Longmans, 1966.
HUSSEY, J. M. *The Byzantine World*, Hutchinson, 1967.
PRESTAGE, F. *The Portuguese Pioneers*, A. &. C. Black, 1966.

Age group 16–18
PROCACCI, G. *A History of the Italian People*, Weidenfeld and Nicholson, 1970
DUNLOP, D. M. *Arab Civilization to A.D. 1500*, Longman, 1971.
LIVERMORE, H. *A History of Spain*, Allen and Unwin, 1966.
LIVERMORE, H. *Italy in the Middle Ages*, Marshall Cavendish, 1970.
NORWICH, J. J. *The Normans of the South*, Longmans, 1967.

Visual aids
Visual Publications filmstrips
The Vikings   Col.
The Crusades   Col.

CLASSICAL STUDIES

Age group 9–12

NEURATH, M. and ELLIS, J. *They Lived like this in Ancient Crete* (also Greece), Macdonald Educ., 1966.

GREEN, P. *The Romans* (Look At Series), Hamish Hamilton, 1963.

TAYLOR, D. *Ancient Greece*, Methuen, 1957.

TAYLOR, D. *Ancient Rome*, Methuen, 1964.

KIRTLAND, G. B. *One Day in Ancient Rome*, Macmillan, 1963.

BAUMANN, H. *The World of the Pharaohs*, Oxford Univ. Press, 1960.

SHEPPARD, E. J. *Ancient Egypt* (Then and There Series), Longmans, 1960.

BOLTON, J. *Ancient Crete and Mycenae*, Longmans, 1968.

SHEPPARD, E. J. *Ancient Athens*, Longmans, 1967.

MITCHISON, N. *Alexander the Great*, Longmans, 1964.

SHERWIN-WHITE, N. *Ancient Rome*, Longmans, 1959.

Age group 12–16

HODGE, P. Aspects of Roman Life: *The Roman House*, Longman, 1971; *The Roman Towns*, Longman, 1972.

MCLEISH, K. (Ed.). Aspects of Greek Life: *The Greek Theatre*, Longman, 1972; *Greek Exploration and Seafaring*, Longman, 1972.

WILLETTS, R. F. *Everyday Life in Ancient Crete*, Batsford, 1969.

QUENNELL, M. J. and C. H. B. *Everyday Things in Ancient Greece*, Batsford, 1954.

GREEN, R. L. *Ancient Greece* (Young Historian Series), Weidenfeld and Nicholson, 1963.

BAUMANN, H. *Lion Gate and Labyrinth*, Oxford Univ. Press, 1967.

PAOLI, U. E. *Rome, Its People, Life and Customs*, Longmans, 1963.

MOSCATI, S. *The World of the Phoenicians*, Weidenfeld and Nicholson, 1968.

WORKMAN, B. K. *They Saw it Happen in Classical Times*, Blackwell, 1964.

COOTES, R. J. and SNELLGROVE, L. E. *The Ancient World*, Longman, 1970.

FIELD, G. L. *The Growth of Civilization*, Macmillan, 1966.

WEBSTER, T. B. L. *Everyday Life in Classical Athens*, Batsford, 1969.

MERCER, C. *Alexander the Great*, Cassel Caravel, 1964.

HAWKES, J. *Pharaohs of Egypt*, Cassel Caravel, 1967.

COTTRELL, L. *Enemy of Rome*, Evans, 1965.

GRANT, M. *Ancient History Atlas 1700 B.C. – A.D. 565*, Weidenfeld & Nicholson, 1971.

Age group 16–18

HEYDEN van der A. and SCULLARD, H. H. *Atlas of the Classical World*, Nelson, 1963.

de BEER, Sir G. *Hannibal: The Struggle for Power in the Mediterranean*, Thames and Hudson, 1969.

FINLEY, M. I. *The Ancient Greeks*, Pelican, 1966.

CRUICKSHANK, J. E., MERRITT, A. S. and PORTER, J. M. *The Rise of Western Civilization*, Longmans, 1967.

BALSDON, J. P. V. *The Romans*, New Thinkers Library, 1965.

OMAN, Sir C. *A History of Greece*, Longmans, 1968.

BURN, A. R. *History of Greece*, Pelican, 1966.

KITTO, H. D. F. *The Greeks*, Penguin, 1967.

BREASTED, J. H. *Ancient Times: A History of the Early World*, Ginn, 1916.
    (Well worth a search in secondhand shops)

Visual aids
Common Ground filmstrips

Life in Ancient Greece	Col.
Life in Egypt	Col.
Life in Ancient Mesopotamia and Life in Ancient Palestine	Col.

The Growth of Rome	Col.
Life in the Roman Empire	Col.

Encyclopaedia Britannica filmstrips

Ancient Rome	Col.

Educational Productions Limited: filmstrips

The Greeks	Col.
The Romans	Col.
The Times of the Roman Caesars	B/W
Alexander the Great	B/W
Assyria and Babylonia	Col.
Egypt	Col.

Longman filmstrips: Then and There Series:

The Ancient World	Col.

Foundation course: The Cambridge School Classics Project
The Cambridge School Classics Project has developed a classics course entirely in English for pupils of all abilities in the 10–13 age range. The first material published is based on Greek civilization and on the following five themes:

Troy and the Early Greeks
The Gods of Mount Olympus
Greek Religion
Athens, Sparta and Persia
Greek Festivals

The first unit consists of a picture of life at the time of the Trojan War with visual and written material on palaces, ships, seafaring, war and domestic life.

The second unit consists of resource material on the Greek gods dealing with their origins and attributes and some of the myths which surround them. The picture cards show how Greek artists and sculptors depicted the gods and include modern artists' impressions and photographs of temples and sites.

Visual Publications filmstrips

Life in Ancient Egypt I	Col.
Life in Ancient Egypt II	Col.
Life in Ancient Greece I	Col.
Life in Ancient Greece II	Col.
The Roman City	Col.
The Roman Villa	Col.
Roman Roads	Col.
Roman Forts and Walls	Col.

LITERATURE

Greek and Roman
Age group 12–16
MCLEISH, K. *Four Greek Plays*, Longmans, 1964.
MCLEISH, K. *The Frogs and Other Plays*, Longmans, 1970
WORMALD, R. D. *The Argonauts*, Longmans, 1962.
WORMALD, R. D. *The Odyssey of Homer*, Longmans, 1958.
PICARD, B. L. *The Iliad of Homer*, Oxford Univ. Press, 1952.
PICARD, B. L. *The Odyssey of Homer*, Oxford Univ. Press, 1962.
MCLEISH, K. *The Story of Aeneas*, Longmans, 1968.

Age group 16–18
GLEN, R. S. *The Two Muses*, Macmillan, 1968.
JOHN, D. A. S. and TURBERFIELD, A. F. *Virgil: The Voyage of Aeneas*, Macmillan, 1968.

Egyptian
KASTER, J. *The Literature and Mythology of Ancient Egypt*, Allen Lane, Penguin, 1970.

BIBLIOGRAPHY

Penguin Classics including

Thucydides	Peloponnesian War
Herodotus	Histories
Homer	Odyssey, Iliad
Virgil	Aeneid
Suetonius	Lives of the Caesars
Pliny	Letters
Camoens	The Ludiads

Visual aids
Encyclopaedia Britannica filmstrips
Iliad   Col.
Odyssey   Col.
Aeneid   Col.
Oedipus the King   Col.
Educational Productions filmstrip
The Odyssey   Col.

MYTHS AND LEGENDS

Age group 9–12
JONES, G. *Scandinavian Legends and Folk Tales*, Oxford Univ. Press, 1956.
KEARY, A. and E. *Heroes of Asgard*, Macmillan, 1905.
GREEN, R. L. *Myths of the Norsemen*, Penguin, 1970.
GREEN, R. L. *Tales of the Greek Heroes*, Penguin, 1970.
GREEN, R. L. *Tales of the Muses Told*, Bodley Head, 1965.
GREEN, R. L. *A Book of Myths*, Dent, 1965.
GRAVES, R. *The Siege and Fall of Troy*, Cassell, 1962.
SERAILLIER, I. *The Gorgon's Head* (Greece), Oxford Univ. Press, 1961.
SERAILLIER, I. *The Clashing Rocks* (Greece), Oxford Univ. Press, 1963.
SERAILLIER, I. *The Way of Danger* (Greece), Oxford Univ. Press, 1962.
CUSCIJA-PRODANOVIC, *Yugoslav Folk Tales*, Oxford Univ. Press, 1957.
DOWNING, C. *Russian Tales and Legends*, Oxford Univ. Press, 1956.
JONES, G. *Scandinavian Legends and Folk Tales*, Oxford Univ. Press, 1956.
DOWNING, C. *Tales of the Hodja*, Oxford Univ. Press, 1964.
      (Folk-tale heroes of the Middle East, the Balkans and Greece.)
NAHMAD, H. M. *The Peasant and the Donkey*, Oxford Univ. Press, 1967.
      (Thirty traditional tales, legends and folk-stories that reflect the charac-
      ter, wisdom and humour of the people of the Near and Middle East.)
PICARD, B. L. *The Iliad of Homer*, Oxford Univ. Press, 1952.
PICARD, B. L. *The Odyssey of Homer*, Oxford Univ. Press, 1952.
PICARD, B. L. *Tales of the Norse Gods and Heroes*, Oxford Univ. Press, 1953.
TAYLOR, N. B. *The Aeneid of Virgil*, Oxford Univ. Press, 1961.

Age group 12–16
GUERBER, H. A. *The Myths of Greece and Rome*, Harrap, 1942.
GARFIELD, L. and BLISHEN, E. *The God Beneath the Sea*, Longman Young Books,
      1970.
GRAVES, R. *The Greek Myths*, Penguin, 1969.
MCGRADY, S. G. *Legends and Myths of Greece and Rome*, Longman, 1970.
WALSH, J. H. *Tales of the Greek Heroes*, Longmans, 1949.
WORMALD, R. D. *The Argonauts*, Longmans, 1962.
SHARWOOD SMITH, J. *Modern Stories of Ancient Greece*, Longman, 1969.

THE SEA, TRAVEL AND NAVIGATION

Titles which are directly related to B.I. Educational Cruises:
DALYELL, T. *Ship School*, Newman Neame, 1963.

CORBRIDGE, S. *We Go in a School Ship*, Harrap, 1967.

JOSEPH, J. and L. O. *Nautical Studies for Educational Cruising*, Sea and Airborne Education, 1968.

Age group 9–12

CAREY, D. *The Ocean Liner*, Ladybird, 1971.

MOODY, J. *Ocean Ships*, Ian Allen Ltd, 1964.

LEE, L. and LAMBERT, D. *The Wonderful World of Transport*, Macdonald, 1969.

DUNN, L. *The Book of Ships*, Macdonald, 1968.

HOPE, R. *Ships* (Junior Heritage Series), Batsford, 1958.

PALMER, M. *Ships and Shipping*, Batsford, 1971.

GOLDSMITH-CARTER, G. *Sailing Ships and Sailing Craft*, Hamlyn, 1969.

WARNER, O. and NIMITZ, C. W. *Nelson and the Age of Fighting Sail*, Cassell, 1963.

WARNER, O. *Captain Cook and the South Pacific*, Cassell, 1964.

DONOVAN, F. *The Vikings*, Cassell, 1965.

BURCHELL, S. *Building the Suez Canal*, Cassell, 1967.

WILLIAMS, J. *The Spanish Armada*, Cassell, 1968.

KNIGHT, F. *Ships* (Now and Then Series), Benn, 1969.

SUTTON, H. T. and LEWIS, G. *Voyages of Adventure* – Bk. 3 (History Workshop Series), Cassell, 1970.

LEWIS, G. *Across the Oceans* – Bk. 4 (History Workshop Series), Cassell, 1970.

KNIGHT, F. *Stories of Famous Explorers by Sea*, Oliver and Boyd, 1964.

Age group 12–16

ELLACOTT, S. E. *The Story of Ships*, Methuen, 1958.

PALMER, M. *Ships and Shipping*, Batsford, 1971.

HOGBEN, *Science and the Navigator*, Brockhampton, 1964.

HOARE, R. J. *Travel by Sea Through the Ages*, A. & C. Black, 1967.

LANDSTROM, B. *The Ship*, Allen and Unwin, 1961.

KNIGHT, F. *A Guide to Ocean Navigation*, Macmillan, 1959.

DODMAN, F. E. *The Observer's Book of Ships*, Warne, 1964.

WYMER, N. *Behind the Scenes on an Ocean Liner*, Dent, 1964.

PENRY-JONES, J. *The Burke Book of Ships and Shipping*, Burke, 1965.

ARMSTRONG, R. *History of Seafaring:*
 Vol. I. *The Early Mariners*, Benn, 1967.
 Vol. II. *The Discoverers*, Benn, 1968.
 Vol. III. *The Merchantmen*, Benn, 1969.

SVENSSON, S. *Sails through the Centuries*, Collier-Macmillan, 1965.

CRONE, G. and KENDALL, A. *The Voyages of Discovery* (Wayland Pictorial Sources Series), Wayland, 1970.

HAMPTON, T. A. *The Sailor's World*, Pan, 1968.

HOPE, R. *Introduction to the Merchant Navy*, S.E.S., 1964.

TOMLINSON, H. M. *Great Sea Stories of all Nations*, Hamlyn, 1967.

HARLAND, S. J. *The Dustless Road* (A career in the Merchant Navy by a Shell Shipmaster), Educational Explorers, 1965.

LLOYD, C. *The British Seaman 1200–1860* (A Social Survey), Paladin Paperbacks, Collins Hardback, 1970.

LLOYD, C. *Greek Exploration and Seafaring*, Longman, 1972.

FINER, L. *Passport to Greece*, Longmans, 1964.

COWIE, E. E. *Living Through History:* No. 9 Discovery, Cassell, 1970.

MOTT, A. S. (Ed.). *Hakluyt's Voyages*, Blackwell, 1929.

Age group 16–18

SLOCUM, J. *Sailing Alone Round the World*, Collier-Mac, 1962.

JOHNSON, L. L. (revised MONCRIEFF, T.). *A First Book of Navigation*, Macmillan, 1966.

TAYLOR, E. G. R. *The Haven Finding Art*, Hollis and Carter, 1971.

BIBLIOGRAPHY

DURELL, L. *Bitter Lemons* (Cyprus), Faber, 1957.
DURRELL, L. *Reflections on a Marine Venus* (Rhodes), Faber, 1953.
DURRELL, L. *Prospero's Cell* (Corfu), 1945.
LIDDELL, R. *Byzantium and Istanbul,* Cape, 1956.
LIDDELL, R. *The Morea,* Cape, 1958.
EVANS, I. O. *Exploring the Earth,* Hutchinson, 1961.

FISHING

ALEXANDER, M. *Behind the Scenes with a Fishing Fleet,* Dent, 1965.
(A comprehensive survey of the modern fishing industry on deep sea fishing.)

SEA FOOD

DAVIDSON, A. *Mediterranean Sea Food,* Penguin, 1972.
(The first section consists of illustrated lined drawings and a description of the edible sea creatures of the Mediterranean.

The second section contains over 200 recipes from Malaga, Sicily, the Dalmatian coast, Corfu, Istanbul, the Turkish Black Sea coast, Alexandria and Bizerta.)

Visual aids
Encyclopaedia Britannica filmstrips
The Age of Exploration   Col.

RELIGION

Age group 9–12
THOMSON, R. W. *People and Lands of the Bible,* Hulton, 1965.
CRABB, E. W. *Living in Old Testament Days,* E. J. Arnold, 1962.
CRABB, E. W. *Living in New Testament Days,* E. J. Arnold, 1962.

Age group 12–16
COUTTS, J. J. *Prophets and Kings of Israel,* Longman, 1969.
DAWSON, L. *The History and Religion of Israel,* Evans, 1968.
BOUQUET, A. C. *Everyday Life in Old Testament Times,* Batsford, 1953.
BOUQUET, A. C. *Everyday Life in New Testament Times,* Batsford, 1953.
JONES, C. *Old Testament Illustrations,* Oxford Univ. Press, 1971.
BALY, D. *The Geography of the Bible,* Lutterworth, 1957.
KOTKER, N. *The Holy Land in the Time of Jesus,* Cassell Caravel, 1968.
KOTKER, N. *The Rise of Islam,* Cassell Caravel, 1969.
KOTKER, N. *The Rise of Christianity,* Marshall Cavendish, 1969.
ROWLEY, H. H. *The Teach Yourself Bible Atlas,* E.U.P., 1960.

Age group 16–18
ALLEGRO, J. M. *The Dead Sea Scrolls,* Penguin, 1956.
BOUQUET, A. C. *Comparative Religion,* Penguin, 1969.
FRAZER, J. G. *The Golden Bough,* Macmillan, 1962.
JAMES, E. O. *History of Religions,* E.U.P., 1965.
ANDERSON, B. W. *The Living World of the Old Testament,* Longmans, 1967.
MEINARDUS, OTTO F. A. *St. Paul in Greece,* Lycabettus Press, 1971.

Party Leaders
BROWNRIGG, R. *Come and See:* For pilgrims and leaders of pilgrims. Darton, Longman and Todd, 1968.
(Some chapters are likely to be of interest to Party Leaders visiting the Holy Land.)

Visual aids

Common Ground filmstrips

Islam	B/W
The World of the New Testament	Col.
Introduction to World Religions	Col.

Educational Productions Limited: filmstrips

The Dead Sea Scrolls	Col.
Assyria and Babylonia	Col.
Egypt	Col.
The Spread of the Church	Col.
The Ministry of Christ	Col·
New Testament Times	Col.

Visual Publications filmstrips

Bible Life:	Col.

    The Shepherd
    The Fisherman
    The Farmer
    Home-life
    The Synagogue
    Trades and Trading
    Inns and Travelling

FURTHER INFORMATION

Detailed information on the books and visual aids listed may be obtained from publishers' catalogues or from the local branch of the County or Public Library, school suppliers and booksellers.

Other sources of information include:

The School Library Association,
Premier House,
150 Southampton Row,
London WC1 5AR.

The National Book League,
7 Albemarle Street,
London W.1X. 4BB.

The National Committee for Audio-Visual Aids in Education,
33 Queen Anne Street,
London W.1M. OAL.

who provide a Visual Education National Information Service for Schools (V.E.N.I.S.S.) and publish a national catalogue of films, filmstrips, slides, overhead projector transparencies, casette loop films, wall charts, records and tapes for Education. The productions of all companies producing material for educational purposes are included to enable teachers to select the most appropriate visual aid on any topic without searching through a number of separate catalogues.

Organisations specialising in particular fields include:

EVASS,
7 Woodhayes Road,
Wimbledon,
London S.W.19.
    Specialise in classical studies.

Visual Publications,
108 High Street,
Kensington,
London W.8. 6BB
    Specialise in slides and filmstrips mainly on art including classical and modern artists.

The London Planetarium Bookshop,
Marylebone Road,
London N.W.1.
Offers books, maps, visual aids and colour transparencies on astronomy
and space.

Sea and Airborne Education,
Lorengau Cottage,
Forest Green,
Dorking,
Surrey.
Publishers of Nautical Studies for Educational Cruising by Joyce and
Lionel O. Joseph 1968 (supplied direct).

Keramos Guides available from:
Lycabettus Press,
39 Dimokritou, Athens 136, Greece,
publish guides on:
Museums of Athens; Sparta; Kerkyra; Nafplion; Asine; Tiryns; Byzantine;
Athens; Delphi; Epidaurus; Pylos.